The LIGHT OF THE WORLD

DAILY MEDITATIONS
FOR ADVENT AND CHRISTMAS

PHYLLIS ZAGANO

TWENTY-THIRD
PUBLICATIONS

TWENTY-THIRD PUBLICATIONS
1 Montauk Avenue, Suite 200, New London, CT 06320
(860) 437-3012 » (800) 321-0411 » www.twentythirdpublications.com

ISBN: 978-1-62785-212-8
Library of Congress Catalog Card Number: 2016909031
Printed in the U.S.A.

A Division of Bayard, Inc.

For My Family

Each year on June 24, around the time of the summer solstice, the church celebrates the feast of John the Baptist. Just a few days earlier, the longest day of the year marks the earth's midpoint between darkness and light. From John's feast onward, days become shorter and daylight decreases. The world slowly moves to a deeper quiet, toward a winter slumber.

John knew he must decrease so that Christ may increase. He gives us good advice. So too must we accept our need for deeper quiet, for silence, and for a lessening as we await in hope the coming of Christ.

At the beginning of Advent, as we prepare for the coming weeks of deeper darkness, we see the earth slow its rhythm. Skies cloud and darken. The winter solstice, the shortest and darkest day of the year will soon arrive.

Although we know more darkness is coming, we know as well nature promises more light, at least in a few weeks' time. The light must decease before it again increases in the regular rhythm of the skies and earth. So too with us. As we look toward more light, and as we prepare for the coming of Christ, we can think of how we might decrease so that the light of Christ may increase both in our lives and in the world.

I think we all know how hard it is to "decrease." Not long ago, Pope Francis chided us all for wanting to achieve some special recognition, some accounting of our worth, by counting how many internet friends or contacts or hits we have. The false sense of security we gain by these electronic means of validation blocks true light—about ourselves and our relationships. How is it we prefer a screen to people? How is it we think sheer numbers can count our worth?

The Advent project, like any other project of the heart, will advance along the lines we set. If we use electronics to reach out to others, fine. If we use them to hide, and/or to move us along in some fantasy world, we are damaging our very selves and seriously endangering our abilities to see the Christ—in the world, in others, and, most importantly, in ourselves.

New media do not present the only darkness. We know too well the ancient list: anger, envy, gluttony, greed, lust, pride, and sloth. Each of these—called the seven deadly sins or the cardinal sins—is title heading for the smaller, simpler sins of everyday life. No thinking person can be completely and routinely enmeshed in any one of these. No loving person will live without checking against their tendencies daily.

Great literature presents the ways these seven affect the human project. When Geoffrey Chaucer wrote *The Canterbury Tales*—tales told by a variety of pilgrims on a pilgrimage to Thomas à Becket's shrine at Canterbury Cathedral—he included only one good clergyman, the parson. In his tale, the parson lays out the points of reference for the soul returning to a life of grace. He says, to the other pilgrims and implicitly to us, that they and we all need penitence, that they and we, each and all, need contrition of the heart, confession of the mouth, and satisfaction for our faults. Such would be the order, and such would be the requirements for every life. Chaucer has use for only one member of the clergy—the parson. He has good advice.

Will Chaucer's advice, conveyed through The Parson's Tale, take root in our hearts this Advent? We can drive ourselves blindly in one direction or another, perhaps in the dim light of evening or in the increasing dark of night. The more we ignore the small tic within that points to the distant relative of one or another of the major faults we know about, the more we will move into a darkness, into a realm of self-involvement and deceit.

Then Advent comes along and calls us to remember that because the dark exists, so also we can know the light, and perhaps even know it more brightly when it comes.

These Advent reflections reflect our natural longing for the light. Like John, we can will ourselves to become quieter, slower even, pointing to the Christ who is to come. Like the pilgrims with the parson, we can look within for ways to make our own hearts and minds more transparent, more open, more accepting of the light.

Where do we go from here?

Year A: ISAIAH 2:1–5; ROMANS 13:11–14; MATTHEW 24:37–44

Year B: ISAIAH 63:16B–17, 19B; 64:2–7;

1 CORINTHIANS 1:3–9; MARK 13:33–37

YEAR C: JEREMIAH 33:14–16; 1 THESSALONIANS 3:12—4:2;

LUKE 21:25–28, 34–36

The days are coming, says the Lord, when I will fulfill the
promise... JEREMIAH 33:14

Promises are delicate things. We have all made promises and
kept them. We have made promises we have broken. So too
we have had promises made to us that others did not keep.
Sometimes we can make excuses, for ourselves or for others.
We (or they) forgot. We (or they) just could not do it.

Sometimes we know the awful truth. We (or they) lied.

When people grow up in situations where promises are
never kept, it is difficult for them to learn to trust; it is hard for
them to hear a promise and expect it to be kept.

But Advent is the time for hope in promises, for hope and
trust in the promise that Christ is coming, to our homes and
lives, to our hearts and minds. Of course, he is already here.
But there is the special sense of waiting, quietly, in the dark, for
Christ in Christmas to enlighten us.

We quiet ourselves and wait.

But even now, the first day of Advent, the outside world is in
a pre-Christmas frenzy. At every turn someone or something is

1

urging us to get out there and shop, shop, shop. The little trap that advertising sets is real. Remember, we are all in the dark in one way or another. We are all wanderers. We all look for something to brighten the way, to bring us joy.

We long for something real, something to hold on to, but the externals of power and possessions do not satisfy the longing. No matter how much we accumulate, there is something else we need. The car must be bigger, the clothing must be newer, the television, the iPad, the cruise—whatever bauble or trinket catches our eye—all these beckon as answers to the longing.

It's not going to work. As God's creations, we can only find security in God's care. As Christians, we must constantly look for the Christ—the Christ who comes to us every single day in new and sometimes startling ways. We can see, if we look gently enough, Christ in all things. Yet even when we see Christ all around us it is too easy to withdraw into our own ways of being dark, of being empty in the wrong ways, of being alone in narcissistic solitude. From these, from emptiness without hope, from solitude that engages us alone, the coming light calls us to escape.

There are two parts to the exercise. First, we must believe that there will be light. Next, we must open our eyes to see it.

Too many times we waste time wandering around in the dark. Too many times we close our eyes to what is coming. We need to believe God's promise that the light will come.

A GRACE FOR TODAY

Lord, give me the grace to open my eyes to belief.

A time to believe

ISAIAH 2:1–5 OR ISAIAH 4:2–6; MATTHEW 8:5–11

"Lord, I am not worthy to have you enter under my roof."

MATTHEW 8:8

Advent is a time when we need to hope, certainly in God. I think first, however, we need to take stock in and really believe in ourselves.

Yes, like the centurion in today's gospel, we are not worthy to have the Lord come "under our roof." But in a very real and honest way we are actually very worthy to have the Lord come to us. In fact, one of the greatest challenges of Christian life is to allow ourselves to believe we are worthy of God's love, to believe we are worthy of the fact that Christ came into our world for us—really and personally—and that God loves us just the way we are.

So when we find ourselves not believing in that fact, we begin to get down on ourselves. Soon the season turns sour. Nothing is quite right. This one or that one did not sit next to me at lunch. She or he did not walk with me that day. I cannot get an appointment, a date, a time to get together with someone I truly want to see. So the spindle turns and pretty soon we are caught in a web of our own creating. We do not believe, first of all, in ourselves, and very soon we forget that we are God's precious creations and worthy of love—of others and of God. That is a huge realization, and one we need to hang on to.

Even if the deep and personal knowledge that we are God's

3

precious creations becomes our own at some time of deep prayer or consolation, it can slip away in an instant when we feel abandoned somehow by someone else, especially by a person we love.

Not long ago, Macy's took for its Christmas theme the word "Believe." In huge white script, "Believe" wrapped itself around boxes and bags, even around parts of the store.

When you think of it, it's not a bad recommendation. We need to believe. We need to believe in God's promise, and we need to believe in ourselves. If we believe in ourselves, when we say "Lord, I am not worthy to have you enter under my roof," we are both stating a fact and asserting our dignity, not asserting that we are worthless. We are in no way equal to God, but as God's beautiful creations we are worthy of receiving him.

That can be a difficult lesson for just about anyone. Somewhere in our minds a difficult memory took up permanent residence years ago. Now, every so often it taunts us with evil's equivalent of the schoolyard chant: "You're ugly and your mother dresses you funny." There is no getting away from it. The memory is ours. It is our own, deep, personal history. As it worms its way into our minds, we feel less and less worthy. The memory is often not that easy to dismiss. But dismiss it we must, sometimes with the graced assistance of a spiritual director or professional counselor, or both. We cannot allow anything to turn us away from God's love for us as his perfect creations, deserving of love in every way.

As we wait this hopeful season, we can consider and pray deeply for the understanding that God has made us and loves us and cares for us.

A GRACE FOR TODAY

Lord, give me the grace to believe in your love for me.

Peace can enter our hearts

ISAIAH 11:1–10; LUKE 10:21–24

He shall judge the poor with justice and decide aright
for the land's afflicted....Then the wolf shall be a guest
of the lamb, and the leopard shall lie down with the kid.

ISAIAH 11:4, 6

Today Isaiah speaks beautifully about God's promise of the one to come, the one who will be filled with the Spirit of the Lord. The promise is for our world today, not for some ancient desert in our imagination.

I think there is genuine excitement in today's readings. The prophet says the one who is to come will be filled with what we know as the gifts of the Holy Spirit: wisdom, understanding, counsel, knowledge, fortitude, piety, and fear of the Lord. Can there be any more hope-filled words?

As God's Spirit rests on Jesus and enters the world through him, we know these promises are real: "the wolf shall be a guest of the lamb, and the leopard shall lie down with the kid." Even so, we ask: When? Where?

We live in a world of constant tragedy. Every single day, it seems, there is another mass death: from war, from disease, from individual acts of evil. Our hearts break as we see the pictures and hear the sounds of so many suffering people. Everybody and everything seems to be at war.

As we await Christ's coming this year, I think there are three levels of war we need to pray about. There is of course the war between nations, among peoples who seek each other's property and power. There are as well the wars between individuals, the private disagreements that fester and spill over to angry exchanges, sometimes even to fistfights and hair-pulling, both real and metaphorical. Then there is the war within our own hearts. It is a very real thing to have opposing ideas collide in our minds.

What to do?

I think the natural reaction to national wars far away is to shake our heads and thank God it is not here, not in my country. But in a very real way, war is in everyone's country. If the bombs and rockets don't fall and explode in our own downtown, they are surely falling in someone else's. And they were paid for by somebody's taxes. So the exploding metal thousands of miles away obliterates money—tax money—that might have fed the hungry child or helped to settle a refugee. The dust and dirt a bomb throws in the air will hurt someone, eventually even us as it clogs the lungs and stunts the growth of someone who might have grown to cure a dread disease.

So too with interpersonal disagreements that spill anger into the air. The toxic waste they leave infiltrates whole communities. People can no longer live together, work together, eat together, even pray together.

When we live in these environs it is all too easy for evil to seep into our minds and disturb our peace. We choose one side or the other. We agree with one or the other in warfare large and small. We defend one or the other without seeking real peace or justice. Yet our faith combines with Scripture here to teach on many levels at once.

Maybe our best response is to begin by trying to work peace

between some warring factions in our own hearts, so as to make us more peaceful inhabitants of the planet.

Lord, give me the grace to seek peace in myself.

Enough for everyone

ISAIAH 25:6–10A; MATTHEW 15:29–37

Jesus summoned his disciples and said, "My heart is moved with pity for the crowd, for they have been with me now for three days and have nothing to eat. I do not want to send them away hungry."...They all ate and were satisfied.

MATTHEW 15:32, 37

The territory around the Sea of Galilee can be very unforgiving. The hills are quite steep in many places, the vegetation is rough scrub, the sun sears the skin in the hot seasons, and rain deadens the mind when winter winds blow through the land. In this gospel, the crowds have come to listen to the great preacher, the one they heard about, perhaps in the village, perhaps on the lakeshore. He has a message they all hunger for.

But we need to pay attention to where they are in time and space. The crowds before Jesus are out in the open, exposed to the elements on a hillside in Palestine. They did not come by bicycle or car. They came on foot. Some may have walked for a day—as much as twenty or twenty-five miles. They are surely tired, and quite probably hungry.

So Jesus's first concern is for their physical security. They have to eat.

Many years ago I taught an 8:00 A.M. class. One semester, that class was popular with the university's basketball team. These were the days before students seemed to have water bottles or coffee cups permanently affixed to their hands. I noticed that this crowd—mostly boys—was particularly inattentive. So I asked: Have you eaten breakfast? The perhaps predictable answer came from most of them: "Uh, no."

It was pretty obvious that not much would be going on in their heads if they had not eaten, but unlike Jesus I could not then and there provide a meal. I could only provide a requirement: eat breakfast before class.

You know, it worked.

My short tale echoes the truth of the gospel passage: we cannot hear God's word if we are in physical distress.

But today's reading is about so much more. Christ's food here is for both the body and the soul. As in the passage, we receive all we need when we need it, and we really should not fear it will not come again. God's bounty is not like an apple pie that, once eaten, is no more. There is always more to hear from God; there is always more to receive from Christ.

We often have a hard time believing this, especially in the pre-Christmas frenzy when there seems to be more to do and less time to do it in, and as days grow shorter and the light grows dim. I think the analogy is real: we know what it means to hear Christ's word, to feel God's touch. But when we are really or metaphorically hungry, we have trouble receiving that word and that touch.

The answer to the problem given by St. Ignatius, founder of the Society of Jesus (Jesuits), is to store up consolations in the face of desolation. That sounds good—like a little chipmunk we pack away good memories like nuts hidden in a tree stump—but it is not the easiest thing in the world. While we can remember the summer-like warmth of graced moments, we are not always sure they will come around again when life gets chilly. In fact, sometimes we feel so terribly empty, we wonder if we ever knew God.

Advent is a time to throw off all that and get rid of the doubts, the fears, and the conviction that never again will we feel the sweetness of God's embrace.

Christ will not allow us to go hungry.

A GRACE FOR TODAY
Lord, give me the grace to not be frightened about my needs.

Is God my foundation?

Isaiah 26:1–6; Matthew 7:21, 24–27

*"Everyone who listens to these words of mine and acts on them
will be like a wise man who built his house on rock."* MATTHEW 7:24

You have to love Jesus' metaphors. We know how this story ends: no foundation, no house. Whether it is built on bad mountainside soil or on the sandy beach near the water, eventually a house doesn't stand a chance against the elements. The foundation is the key to it all, and something solid is the answer. In Jesus' time that would be rock; nowadays it is more likely concrete blocks. No matter which, it had better be solid.

We are always building. We build homes. We build a network of friends and associates; we build a web of memories and of customs. These bring some measure of the security we so long for: the shelter of a solid place in which to live, the shelter of a loving circle of friends, the shelter of the memories of a life well lived. Each and all contribute to our mental health and spiritual welfare. Each and all help us to know ourselves as secure.

If we see God in all things—another recommendation of St. Ignatius—we can be grateful for our homes, our friends, our life experiences as expressions of God's care for us. However, if we see everything as a required gift to us, we are sliding off our own foundations into ruin.

The world does not owe us a living. Such an attitude will soon turn us inward and eventually create an interior nastiness that is very hard to shake. We owe all we have and are to God, and so our every act must be directed in gratitude for the gifts.

I have spent a good part of my life near a sandy beach. Builders do all sorts of things to stabilize the buildings. Years ago they pounded locust pilings into the sand and sat houses on top of them. More recently they dug the kinds of concrete foundations common in other areas. The scary part is that a good-sized storm can knock a house off its foundation, no matter wood or concrete.

Just so with us. We do intend to live our lives with God as our foundation, and we build that foundation on the words of Christ. We do gratefully receive the priceless gift of God's love—the teachings of Christ. But sometimes we forget and think we did it all ourselves. Sometimes we think, as I suggested just above, it is all about us.

Of course it is not.

The idea that it is can create a very big storm.

The rock-solid foundation of our lives is our relationships. There is no safety within walls—whether those of home or those of selfishness—when the world outside needs us. In fact, we build the foundations of our lives outside, among the others, by participating in the society we live in. So we can, as we have time, participate in a civic activity—a school board or a library committee meeting, or voting in a special election. We can, as we have time, carry the works of mercy to another—we visit the sick; we comfort the forlorn; we smile at the stranger.

There is a very interesting thing that happens when we take the gospel as the rock on which we set the foundation of our lives. It is often called happiness; it is always called hope.

A GRACE FOR TODAY

Lord, help me rest my life on the foundation of your Word.

Recognize light

ISAIAH 29:17–24; MATTHEW 9:27–31

"Do you believe that I can do this?" "Yes, Lord," they said
to him. Then he touched their eyes and said, "Let it be done for
you according to your faith." MATTHEW 9:28-29

The first week of Advent is ending, and already we cannot
see where we are going. Each night the cities and towns get
brighter and noisier, as lights flash and carols blare. We know in
our hearts that Christmas is about the coming of Christ, but the
startling lights and sounds around us turn our minds in another
direction.

We are in danger of going blind.

Physical blindness, like that of the men in today's gospel, is a
terrifying prospect. We cannot imagine our world without light,
especially now as Christmas trees pop up in town squares and
sparkling displays shine in department store windows. But too
much light is blinding.

What blinds us right now? What can we not see in our own
lives? We live in hope for the coming of the Christ, but we may
not be able to open our eyes to greet him. Is Christ the child
(abandoned and alone in a dumpster)? Is Christ the teenager
(wide-eyed at a first try of drugs)? Is Christ the neighbor (an-
noyingly cloying, and with a barking dog)? Is Christ the old
man (smelling of urine and garlic)?

The duty of each of us, of every Christian, is to become another Christ, but I think too often we look to a far-off sterilized Christ of our own imaginations. That Christ we can control. But in fact, the hardest Christ to recognize is the Christ in the news or on the train or even right next door.

There is another step, however. Before we try to see the Christ in others, we must recognize the Christ within ourselves. We cannot close our eyes to God's life within us. To do so threatens our ability to believe in the genuine fact of the Wholly Other, whose light really is too bright for us to receive and whose light might plunge us into an unfamiliar darkness.

That is the challenge and that is the risk. God's piercing light can blind us, temporarily, because we cannot stand to look at what it shows within our hearts. Yet that kind of blindness is both ailment and cure.

The analogy to physical blindness works very well here. We fear blindness, yes, but we spend some goodly time closing off natural light. We close our eyes in trust for large amounts of time—surely when we sleep, often when we pray, or rest, or are in deep thought.

When God's light pierces through whatever veil we try to put before us, we are plunged into a different sort of dark. We can accept it if we wish. We can accustom ourselves to the light and gradually see what the Lord is showing us.

The problem here is one of trust. We only need to ask. Jesus asks the two blind men, just as he asks each one of us: "Do you believe that I can do this?" What do we answer? What do we say in prayer? Do we believe? Can we let go of all the false lights that claim to light our way? Can we sit in the "dark" of God's piercing light and ask for forgiveness, for healing, for deeper knowledge of God's love?

We receive God's piercing light best in a darkness of our own creating. Just for today, maybe we can leave aside one distraction. One fewer television program or telephone call or newspaper story will create more space for God's light.

Lord, help me not fear the darkness of your great light.

Help me, O Lord

Isaiah 30:19–21, 23–26; Matthew 9:35—10:1, 5a, 6–8

He will be gracious to you when you cry out,
as soon as he hears he will answer you. The Lord will give you
the bread you need and the water for which you thirst.

ISAIAH 30:19-20

Sometimes God seems very distant. While Advent is a time of hopeful waiting for the Lord, it is also a time of deep sorrow and sadness for those who are closing a year filled with loss.

Being human means needing the help of others. Often, we do not like to think we need anyone else. The trap of self-sufficiency is wide and welcoming; it encourages us to "go it alone." Of course that only digs us in deeper.

Many years ago I worked at a hotel pool as a lifeguard. Day after day I sat and watched the swimmers. Only rarely did I need to pull someone out, away from danger. Usually folks accepted the help and were grateful for the assist. But I think, as any lifeguard will tell you, there is always one.

My "one" came on a day off at the beach. I was already out beyond the breakers when I noticed someone in trouble—I forget exactly who, but I know it was a man—and I went to help. Not only was he in trouble, he began to try to climb up on me, as if I was some stairway to safety. I had to slap him—perhaps I even punched him—to bring him to his senses and then get him closer to the shore. Once the lifeguard on duty saw what was going on, he came to the rescue and we got the failing swimmer to the beach.

He was fine.

He never thanked me.

On the one hand, you don't really need thanks in situations like that. On the other, what was his number? I have often thought back to that summer day at the beach, and I wonder if the problem was that here he was, a man, being pulled out of danger by some, well, by some girl. Of course, it may have been something else. Of course, he was stunned. Of course, he could have simply forgotten.

But I think a man being slapped around in public by a girl—I was, after all, only a teenager—was something he could not accept. I think he was embarrassed.

What does this have to do with the gospel? We have God's promise here, relayed as it is through Isaiah: as soon as the Lord hears you cry out you will be answered. You will get what you need.

This cuts both ways. Yes, God will put someone or something in your path and things will turn out all right. You will get the bread. You will get the water. You will get exactly what is your need.

But you need to accept it. You need to take the hand that is offered to you, be it male or female. You need to hear the kind word, no matter who passes it along. You need to accept the fact that you cannot—in fact you should not—go it alone all the time.

And with that realization, a very interesting thing happens. We begin to understand—for the first time or again—that the Lord can bind up the wounds of his people only with our help. Once we can accept help, we are capable of offering it to others. And once we are especially attentive to others' sorrows, when we notice they are sad and listen to their grief, we become part of God's promise. We become agents of God's hope and of God's help that circles back to us when we need it.

A GRACE FOR TODAY
Lord, grant me the grace to see the other's need.

He is coming!

Year A: Isaiah 11:1–10; Romans 15:4–9; Matthew 3:1–12

Year B: Isaiah 40:1–5, 9–11; 2 Peter 3:8–14; Mark 1:1–8

Year C: Baruch 5:1–9; Philippians 1:4–6, 8–11; Luke 3:1–6

A voice cries out: In the desert prepare the way of the Lord!
Make straight in the wasteland a highway for our God!

ISAIAH 40:3

The cry of John the Baptist rings out in the desert. He is coming. The One is coming. The One will be here soon!

The Judean desert is a forbidding place. I always thought the desert was something like Jones Beach on Long Island, with nice soft white sand. It is not. The desert where John preached has the look and feel of crumbling concrete as you walk across it. Its hard and unforgiving dirty tan surface kicks back clouds of dust and clods of dry earth as you walk. Winds suddenly whistle from somewhere. Behind? Ahead? And it is dry, as dry as anything you can imagine.

John lived in the desert. Some say he was part of the community around Qumran. They say the famous Dead Sea Scrolls turned up in the Qumran Caves in the Judean Desert of the West Bank, Palestine, because a shepherd boy threw a stone into a cave and heard an unusual sound. They say he threw that stone, and rather than a clunk or plunk, he heard the sound of clay pots breaking. That is the story, at least. In any event, archaeologists found scrolls with texts of the Hebrew Bible. Some scholars argue other scrolls found there evidence the earliest Christian community.

John was present, there or elsewhere. There may have been more water around in John's time, but you can tell from the topography that locusts and honey would be a good meal, if you could find them.

So, we have in our imagination wild-eyed John, proclaiming that he is not the one, but that the One who is to come is really coming.

Yawn. One more nut case. Who can believe this John? What is he telling us to do? How are we to prepare the "way of the Lord"? How are we to make straight a highway in a wasteland?

Well, maybe the wasteland is in our own hearts. We are "dry" and "empty" and "abandoned." Sometimes—not always—but sometimes, we create our own wastelands; we create our own interior deserts in any one of a hundred, no, a thousand, ways. We fill our senses unnecessarily with food, drink, entertainment, talk. All these and more fill wondrous needs. All these and more can dry up the gentle springs of grace that irrigate the deserts of our hearts.

I think that is what John is telling us here, now, two thousand years after he first announced the coming of the Christ. When I hear John shout "make straight the way of the Lord," I do of course recall that desert near Qumran. I remember the dry ground and the dry air. But I recall as well the fact that I can do something here and now to bring refreshment to the dryness, to feed my heart and let myself shout out joyfully with John: He is coming! The Christ is coming!

Of course, there always is the chance that I may not. Like others grown lukewarm, I may ignore John's shouts or eventually dismiss them from belief. That is the daily challenge for any Christian.

Maybe we should look at it this way, with a nod to Pascal's wager. If John is wrong and there is no Christ, but I proclaim Christ's coming anyway, I have lost nothing. But if John is right and I do not believe, I have lost everything.

A GRACE FOR TODAY

Lord, grant me the grace to believe you will come to my desert.

The promise

ISAIAH 35:1–10; LUKE 5:17–26

Be strong, fear not! Here is your God,....he comes to save you.

ISAIAH 35:4

I do not think there is any other season when the prophecy of Isaiah so lovingly pierces our hearts. God has made us a promise, and Isaiah is God's witness to it. Our dear and loving God, Jesus the Christ, has come to save us.

Did the paralyzed man in Luke's gospel today know that? He must have had some understanding of the Christ, and surely his friends believed the promise. And what friends they were! They could not get in the front door, so they climbed to the roof and lowered him in on a stretcher.

Can you imagine? Here is the teacher, Jesus, with people surrounding him. They sit and listen to his word. He is the spring of refreshing water flowing into the desert of their lives. He brings them hope. Then, all of a sudden, this paralyzed fellow is lowered down into their midst.

Do you think it disrupted things a little? Were they angry? Were they surprised? I think I would be.

We have all had unexpected visitors, although probably not through the roof. Sometimes people's needs overcome their natural reticence to impose on us. So they come. I know I have done it myself, and you probably have as well. I have asked for rides to work—when my car was down or once when I was recovering from hand surgery and was not allowed to drive. I have asked to stay with friends—when there was no hotel around or when I just plain did not have the money for one. These things and more can cause a twinge of embarrassing memory, but one packed with gratitude for others' generosity.

Just so, the paralyzed man and his friends show up in the middle of Jesus' preaching. Right there, the paralyzed man comes down through the roof near Jesus. And, what does Jesus do? He cures the man. He stops what he is doing. Right there, in the middle of everything and everyone, he cures him. Then, he says to the others: "your sins are forgiven you."

Amazing! Imagine what the friends were thinking. Perhaps one had this thought cross his mind: he is telling us it is OK to disrupt his preaching. Perhaps another scratched his head, then recognized he did indeed believe that Jesus was the Christ and that he could heal and forgive sins.

There must have been some confusion about the cure because finally Jesus tells the paralyzed man to pick up his mat and walk. And he did. I can think of no more astonishing event. Neither could they. The whole crowd of them went off glorifying God.

We can look at these events with somewhat jaded eyes, but imagine watching them on television. Let them become quite real. You know yourself, whenever there is a miraculous rescue: a child is pulled from a well; a firefighter blown out of a window lands safely; a horrific car accident ends with no one hurt. Who gets credit? No matter their religion, people uniformly attribute miracles to God.

So, why wouldn't the people who saw the paralyzed man pick up his mat do the same? Why wouldn't these people see that Jesus' words are those of God come to save them?

I think we try sometimes (or more than sometimes) to credit coincidence or chance for things that really have no earthly reason. We don't really want to think too deeply about the power of God, perhaps because that power is so terrifying.

That is the challenge. That is the promise.

A GRACE FOR TODAY

Lord, grant me the grace to know you come to heal.

Comfort

ISAIAH 40:1–11; MATTHEW 18:12–14

Comfort....Here is your God!....Like a shepherd he feeds
his flock; in his arms he gathers the lambs, carrying them
in his bosom, and leading the ewes with care.

ISAIAH 40: 1, 10, 11

Around this time during Advent, the church changes vestments from purple to white for one day to honor the feast of the Immaculate Conception of Mary, the Mother of Jesus. This feast is dedicated to the teaching that Mary was born sinless. Many people confuse it with the feast of the Annunciation, which recalls when the angel Gabriel told Mary she would become the mother of God.

There is a lot of other confusion about Mary. There is a heresy called "quaternity" that counts Mary in with the Trinity, making the Godhead four persons, not three. I don't think we need to add Mary to the Trinity to see her loving kindness in the Godhead, or to see the Godhead reflected in her.

I have always thought of Mary as watching over me. As I grew up, no matter where I lived, I had the same small statue of Mary at the head of my bed. It did not glow in the dark; it was not made of china or glass. It was, and still is, just a little plastic statue of Our Lady. It sits beside my bed even as I write.

For me, Mary is a loving mother: forgiving and consoling, tender and compassionate. The word I attach to her is "comfort." Comfort is what Isaiah promises from God, and Mary embodies that comfort.

Whether today or any other day, I think that is the key in our lives with God. Comfort is what God brings and comfort is what God promises. Comfort is what we need. Comfort is what we hope for.

We all suffer trials. During this holy and hopeful season, we may suffer one or another more than usual. These days, some people mourn a death more deeply. These days, some people feel their own diminishment in aging more keenly. These days, some people wonder why the cheer of the season does not settle into their homes and hearts.

Yet God's comfort is available to us all. I know myself I sometimes forget to ask for it. Mary, around now celebrated as born sinless, is first and foremost a dear mother to us. She joins our Lord in comforting us in our losses, in our diminishment, in our inability to receive the coming joy.

But today and every day, we have God's promise that our journey will be marked out for us and our load will be lightened, if we ask. That is the hard part. I am not saying that God is a global positioning system that dictates our every move. Nor that God will erase our memories. But God will mark the way and ease our burdens. We only have to ask. In all humility we need to ask for direction and for help.

I think the asking is the hard part. I know sometimes it is hard to convince myself that I do not know the way, that I cannot carry my burdens alone. Sometimes, when I neglect to ask for help, I get truly lost.

"Comfort" is the first word in The Messiah, Georg Frideric Handel's famous oratorio that so often echoes in churches and concert halls this season. I try to hold on to that word. No one said life would be easy. But we will not be tried beyond our strength if we ask, and many times the first thing we must ask for is God's comfort.

A GRACE FOR TODAY

Lord, comfort me.

Our strength is in the Lord

ISAIAH 40:25–31; MATTHEW 11:28–30

Jesus said to the crowds: "Come to me, all you who labor and are burdened, and I will give you rest." MATTHEW 11:28

I sometimes think the problem with Advent is that it is just before Christmas. That's a fact, not a joke. The extraordinarily beautiful readings during Advent in the church's daily prayer—in the Liturgy of the Hours and the Liturgy of the Eucharist—get swept aside in the rush of things.

A lot of the pre-Christmas rush is external. Jingle bells start ringing once December rolls around and sometimes even sooner, but some of the rush is internal. For whatever reason, I too often fall into the trap of not lingering with Scripture this holy season, not savoring the words of the prophets and evangelists foretelling and telling the story of Christ.

Every year I say I'll do better. I say I'll pay more attention. I say I'll spend more time with God. Then every year I am making lists during Mass and writing cards instead of praying; I find I am taking on too much, eating too much, and visiting too much.

I have to wonder what I am afraid of. What am I avoiding? Why am I so busy? The fact of the matter is, Advent is only ten days old and already I am tired.

Why?

We all are burdened. We all labor. We all need rest. Can you walk and not grow weary? I can't. Not many people can. Is the burden too heavy? It often is, for me and for you. But when I look at the day, do I find I would not let anyone help?

There is a terrible trap in the spiritual life, and especially around this time of the year. We are busy, truly busy. We have things to do, places to go, people to meet. There are early Christmas parties and late-night shopping expeditions. There are the cards and the letters and the telephone calls. There are all the wonderful experiences of life that crowd out our time of solitude and eat away our time of simplicity before God.

That is the trap. In our busyness we are convinced we are serving others, when it is entirely possible we are only serving ourselves, trying to make ourselves feel good, or better, by somehow connecting with other people. We can confuse this busyness with true dependence on God. In fact, sometimes when we think we are depending on God, we are really only depending on ourselves. We are trying to comfort ourselves.

I've been a professor all my adult life. These beginning weeks of Advent bring term papers and examinations, end-of-year reports and final department meetings. So much of my work cannot be delegated, and work seems to have the ability to fill every available minute in the day. So I am very busy during Advent.

The old adage of "all work and no play" is real, and "all work and no pray" is extra-real these precious days, when every single Scripture passage promises God's comfort and assistance. The important thing is to accept the help that is offered, both from God and from the people who make up the body of Christ. We cannot do it alone. We just can't.

A GRACE FOR TODAY

Lord, grant me the grace to accept help.

Trusting

ISAIAH 41:13–20; MATTHEW 11:11–15

I am the Lord, your God, who grasp your right hand;
It is I who say to you, "Fear not, I will help you." ISAIAH 41:13

The days are getting shorter and darker. There is less light and less warmth. The old hurts of Christmases past rise up to chill us even more.

When I was very young, my grandfather was dying as Christmas approached. I was left at my aunt's home on Christmas Eve. I was in a great panic. What if Santa Claus could not find me? Trying my best to stay awake, I remember sinking into the big blue couch across from the huge Christmas tree in the living room. Maybe I could catch Santa and tell him I was there and not at home.

I could not stay awake.

Somehow I awoke in my own bed in my own house on Christmas. Much to my delight, Santa had found me during the dark night.

We have many fears in the dark nights of the season. Christmas lights and music do not dispel the anxiety that comes upon us. I sometimes think that is why the church puts forth its most consoling Scriptures at this time of year. Yes, Advent is a time of hopeful waiting. Yes, we are patient as we await the Lord. But so much of the waiting is done in the dark. So much of the waiting is done in fear.

What do we fear? We fear death, of course. We fear the natural course of nature because we do not know, really, where it will take us. Illness at this time of the year is particularly difficult, whether our own or that of someone we love. And the nightly news is no help. As if we don't have enough to worry about, the latest tragedy endlessly plays on television and radio.

So fear, like fog, creeps in and overtakes our expectant hope, surrounding it with silence. And we become afraid.

Can we let Isaiah's words rescue us? If we have managed to make a few appointments with ourselves to think and pray about the promise of Christmas, we can take Isaiah's words and hold them close. We can hear God speak: "I am the Lord, your God, who grasp your right hand; It is I who say to you, 'Fear not, I will help you.'"

I just love that image. I just love that feeling. I am small again, afraid as Christmas draws near. But God holds my hand and consoles me.

Ignatian spirituality's teaching that we must store up our consolations for the bad times that will surely come is really good advice. I think again of that little chipmunk preparing in the fall for the dark winter of desolation that will surely come. So, when prayer is cold and God seems far away, consolations of times past can warm us and remind us that even far away, God is there for us.

So it is with these few words from Isaiah. I've used them many times myself. God grasps my right hand; he really does. God says, "Fear not." God promises, "I will help you."

Wow! Of course, the next thing on the list is to believe God's promise.

A GRACE FOR TODAY

Lord, grant me the grace to know you hold my hand today.

31

Paying attention

Isaiah 48:17–19; Matthew 11:16–19

*I, the Lord, your God, teach you what is for your good,
and lead you on the way you should go. If you would hearken to
my commandments, your prosperity would be like a river, and
your vindication like the waves of the sea.* Isaiah 48:17-18

Perhaps you have heard the expression: "his lights are out,"
meaning that he's not paying attention, that he is—metaphorically, at least—somewhere else. It usually means someone is
daydreaming.

Some people tend to daydream a lot, and they do so for
many reasons. Students can build entire castles in their minds,
complete with moats and armored men mounted on mighty
steeds, within the first few moments of a boring lecture. Entire
congregations can shut out the droning pastor within seconds
of his beginning an unprepared homily.

Many, if not most, of us turn our minds to other things
during television commercials, on long bus trips, even in the
shower. Most times we are not daydreaming, but thinking
about what has happened in the past or what might happen
in the future. There is a deep distinction between planning an
event (How much food for the birthday party?) and flat out
daydreaming (If I win the lottery…).

One train of thought is genuine "thinking." Planning a party

takes time and careful consideration of all the moving parts—
the guests, the food, the location, etc. The other is not real.

The distinction applies as well to prayer. We can and often
should get God involved in planning. Not that the Lord has
better ideas about whether chocolate or yellow cake is better.
We have different kinds of planning going on all the time in
our lives. Sitting quietly pondering the future and presenting
options to the Lord is actually quite important. The types of
decisions—large and small—that regularly pop up in our lives
require serious thought and, more often than not, prayer.

In fact, some decisions require hard choices, which is where
the soft and comforting act of daydreaming becomes a bit of
a temptation. Suppose the future promises a new house. It is
useless to daydream away about the house you cannot afford
instead of seriously considering the one you can buy. Holding
off the decision until you win the lottery will not get you anywhere.

While most of us will immediately say, "No, that is not me;
I do not daydream, I live in the real world!" there is a good
chance that if we look at the past month, or week, or even today,
we'll find a moment when we've caught the "if-only" bug and
veered ever so slightly toward daydreams.

So we need to pay attention. Isaiah records God's promise
that if we pay attention, our "prosperity will be like a river."
Pay attention to what? Here, the Lord says it is his "commandments." What are they?

Simply put, God's commandments—if we think of the ten
given to Moses—involve our relations with God, with ourselves, and with others. The important point is that they are all
relational. We are charged with being in relation to God and
others and, as they apply to our relations with ourselves, the

commandments tell us to be other-directed. That is, self-absorption is a non-starter. Yet self-absorption is the first recourse of the daydreamer, for whom no one and no thing (including God) can substitute.

So we need to pay attention.

A GRACE FOR TODAY

Lord, help me to always be present to reality.

Prophecy

SIRACH 48:1–4, 9–11; MATTHEW 17:9A, 10–13

"Elijah has already come, and they did not recognize him but did to him whatever they pleased. So also will the Son of Man suffer at their hands." MATTHEW 17:11-12

Scripture, like life, is sometimes confusing. Today, Jesus explains that John the Baptist is the Elijah preparing the way of the Lord. Sirach addresses Elijah directly: "You were destined, it is written, in time to come to put an end to wrath before the day of the Lord." And Jesus tells his disciples (that includes us) that Elijah has already come.

They all know Elijah. He was a famous prophet, revered even today in Judaism. He performed many miracles in the past, and Jewish tradition says he witnesses all circumcisions and helps solve difficult legal problems. Elijah is also mentioned in Islam's Qur'an. There, as in the Bible's Books of Kings, he is recalled as a great man who preached against Ba'al, or Beelzebub, a wholly negative false god.

But Jesus is not talking about the Elijah of the Old Testament. Gradually, the disciples and we understand Jesus' words. The New Testament Elijah is John the Baptist, who foretold the coming of Jesus. Did anyone recognize John?

And, Jesus says, what they did to John the Baptist they will do as well to the Son of Man, to Jesus.

That's scary. Here we are awaiting the birth of the Child,

and the church presents us with readings reminding us that prophecy is a very dangerous business. John the Baptist died for it. Jesus will die for it. Anyone who takes up the voice of the prophet to speak truth to both the powerful and the powerless will be killed.

So, what are the choices? Do we consecrate ourselves and our lives to the truth? Or do we serve Beelzebub, the lie? Two thousand years later, in our comfortable studies, it is all well and good to dream of the marvelous things we will do and say to testify to the truth. But when someone in power asks for your head on a platter, things get pretty uncomfortable.

In my own work, I have the opportunity to speak in support of the world's voiceless and powerless. I have learned you can become very annoying in this vocation, even and especially when you stick steadfastly to the truth. For example, there is a vicious lie perpetrated by a very few in power that women cannot image Christ. That is because they think if you say a woman can image Christ then you are arguing that a woman can be ordained a priest. Believe me, there are other, stronger arguments to use against women priests.

But powerful people—and they are not all men—bring up this terrible notion whenever they are asked about women in church ministry. In my work, it comes up whenever they are asked about women being restored to the ordained diaconate. To say a woman cannot image Christ is not only wrong; it is sick.

We all image Christ. And we best image Christ when we speak the truth.

That is the problem of Advent. We know who is coming, even as we avoid the fact that the little Child in the manger will grow to be the powerless, powerful Savior of the world. He will live a life of healing and of prophecy, and he will be mistrusted, misunderstood, even hated for it. His gentle words will crash against the many lies of then and now.

Yet it is he, whose birth we await, whom we must learn to follow.

A GRACE FOR TODAY

Lord, grant me the strength to speak the truth.

Rejoice!

Year A: Isaiah 35:1–6a, 10; James 5:7–10; Matthew 11:2–11

Year B: Isaiah 61:1–2a, 10–11; 1 Thessalonians 5:16–24; John 1:6–8, 19–28

Year C: Zephaniah 3:14–18a; Philippians 4:4–7; Luke 3:10–18

When John the Baptist heard in prison of the works
of the Christ, he sent his disciples to Jesus with this question,
"Are you the one who is to come, or should we look for another?"
Jesus said to them in reply, "Go and tell John what you hear
and see: the blind regain their sight, the lame walk, lepers
are cleansed, the deaf hear, the dead are raised, and the
poor have the good news proclaimed to them. And blessed
is the one who takes no offense at me." MATTHEW 11:2-6

John gets a very hopeful message here from his own disciples, again probably part of what we now call the Qumran community, known for the Dead Sea Scrolls. These bits and pieces of Scripture connect us to the people who were waiting for the Lord in an ancient past.

Today in the gospel, John receives some very exciting news—a message from Jesus—in response to his searching question: "Are you the one who is to come?"

The answer, quite simply, is yes.

So the church calls this Third Sunday of Advent Gaudete Sunday. The first word of this Sunday's liturgy is *gaudete*—rejoice! We may hear the Latin echo in the gauzy memory of

years past: "Gaudete in Domino semper: iterum dico, Gaudete."
Rejoice in the Lord always: again, I say rejoice.

It is a day of rejoicing. Some churches still have rose-colored vestments. They are used but twice a year: today and on Laetare Sunday in Lent. The color itself lends joy to the season, a bit of a break in the hopeful uphill hike toward Christmas.

I recall being at a Gaudete Sunday Mass in New York City celebrated by the future Cardinal Archbishop of New York, John J. O'Connor, then an auxiliary bishop in the Military Ordinariate. As he began his homily, he looked down at his vestments and said: "I feel like a dining room table." You couldn't help but laugh. There he was, a newly retired Navy chaplain, dressed in pink brocade. It did seem a little incongruous.

But then again, why not pink—or rose—vestments? Too feminine? Today the church rejoices in the fact that the Savior who will come is really coming, and he is coming for us all, male and female. In each cycle of readings—A, B, and C—today's gospel passage has a note of hope, a bit of light. Yes, this really will happen. Yes, Christ will be born in Bethlehem. And, yes, this really is the Christ promised in Scripture.

I think this is where we get lost, in or out of Advent. We hope for the Christ, but we cannot really believe he will come. So the doubts pile on. What is this foolishness? A Savior? A Savior of the world? Give me a break. No one can straighten out what is going on in the Middle East, or anywhere else—in Africa, in Asia, in South America. Even in North America there are fewer and fewer people looking for the peace of Christ and more and more people looking for guns.

That is the scary part. We say we await the Christ. We say we know he will come. We say we believe in the promise of peace.

But, at the bottom, we are caught up in the fear that it is all fake, it is all a fraud.

Lord, grant me the grace to believe you will come.

FOLLOW THE DAILY READINGS
FOR ADVENT UNTIL DECEMBER 17.

How can you do these things?

NUMBERS 24:2–7, 15–17A; MATTHEW 21:23–27

*When Jesus had come into the temple area, the chief priests
and the elders of the people approached him as he was teaching
and said, "By what authority are you doing these things?
And who gave you this authority?"* MATTHEW 21:23

Do we ever ask him directly? Do we ever ask Jesus how it is he
can do what he does? Do we ever ask him how he is who he is?

I think the deep question we cannot avoid throughout
Advent is the "how?" How is it the Child whom we know is
coming, whom we know will come, can grow, as the Scriptures
tell us, in wisdom, age, and grace to be the Christ? How does
this happen? And, more important, how can we better know
him as he is?

Great writers throughout the centuries have helped us form
answers to the question. One, the Carmelite Saint John of the
Cross, died in mid-December, and in larger or smaller measures
the church usually recognizes his feast during these middling
days of Advent. A constant in the church's commemoration of
John of the Cross is the selection from his Spiritual Canticle
presented in the liturgy of the Office of Readings. John advises
us to "dig deeply" into Christ, telling us "he is like a rich mine
with many pockets containing treasures."

What a beautiful analogy. No matter how many times we
hear Jesus' voice in Scripture, when we hear it again, there is

something fresh, something new. Each time Jesus' words appear in Scripture, there is another turn to what we already know.

In today's readings we await Jesus' answer to a very pressing question: by whose authority do you do these things? Jesus could answer, he could say he is the Son of God, he could say he is the Christ, come to save humanity, but he does not answer his challengers here. He stays silent. Even so, we know on whose authority he does what he does.

Or do we? Do we believe that God grants Jesus his power to teach and to preach, to heal and to console? Do we believe that God can grant these powers? Jesus is, after all, human.

Come to think of it, the human Jesus in Scripture is not all that different from any of us. God calls him to do good. People in authority challenge him. He ignores their challenge. He just does it.

People in authority often challenge what we want to do, including and especially when we want to go against the grain, as it were, and perform a good work that the general society might not fully approve of. Too often we fail to act because we are waiting for someone else to give us permission. But what does permission entail, and do we always need it? Do we need permission to call a friend, or to smile at a stranger, or to take a little quiet time? These may be the easy permissions, or sometimes they may get a little harder. However, the genuinely hard "permissions" involve speaking truth to a power that does not want to listen.

No matter which, we get permission when we accept it. As soon as we recognize within ourselves God's call to live a Christian life, we have permission to live it. God gives us all permission to act as Jesus would, to do as Jesus would to others and to ourselves. And here is where John of the Cross can give us a hand. He is absolutely correct when he says we will never find the end to all the treasures hidden for us in Scripture.

Lord, help me know you more intimately.

Following orders

ZEPHANIAH 3:1–2, 9–13; MATTHEW 21:28–32

Jesus said to the chief priests and the elders of the people: "What is your opinion? A man had two sons. He came to the first and said, 'Son, go out and work in the vineyard today.' The son said in reply, 'I will not,' but afterwards he changed his mind and went. The man came to the other son and gave the same order. He said in reply, 'Yes, sir,' but did not go. Which of the two did his father's will?" MATTHEW 21:28-31

When asked to do what we do not want to do, we can complain or we can comply. Some people do both.

Whenever I hear this gospel passage I think of a colleague of mine, years ago. Whenever there was a function at the university, we were asked to sign up, asked to let the administrators know whether we would be at whatever event—a day for new students, graduation, an alumni gathering—I assume so they could plan for chairs and food.

My colleague always signed up. He never went. He never went to anything, but his name was always on the "attendance list." For the first few times I noticed the discrepancy, I chalked it up to some sudden event that forced his change in plans. But over the years, I realized he attended nothing. Even so, there it was in writing: he planned to do what was asked. And no one seemed to notice that he never did.

Of course, there are many reasons not to attend a function,

but there is an oily residue left to outright lies.

In this gospel, it is the father asking his sons to go to the vineyard. One says yes, and does not go; the other says no and goes. Of course we know the moral of the story, and the way the church has interpreted the father as God and the sons as all of us. Patriarchy aside, it is an interesting comparison. We are asked. We can say "yes" or we can say "no."

What are we asked? That is the never-ending question of discernment. We are constantly faced with choices large and small, and the scale we weigh them on is quiet prayer. The task is to choose the good, and when we have competing goods, we hope we choose what best serves our best selves, as we know ourselves in God's light.

That is called doing the will of God. It has less to do with trudging out to vineyards or attending faculty functions and more to do with self-understanding and self-respect.

One example I have often used when teaching spirituality to undergraduates is the question of discerning vocation. Some things I can eliminate right away. I might like to become a professional musician, but I just don't have the talent. The same with so many other choices life spreads before us. The students understand right way: don't waste your time on what you cannot do. There are ways that we are made and there are ways that we are not.

The mistake is to keep butting our heads against walls too strong to break—walls of time or talent or aptitude—rather than pouring out our lives on what it possible and quite probable. These are, of course, the delicate questions of discernment that cannot be answered completely alone, but the bottom line is at least to recognize that there are things God wants for us and things from which we are protected.

Too often, when we do not get what we want, or when things do not go our way, we cry out to the Lord about "unfairness." I truly believe that eventually we may notice that the hand of God was there, even in our pain, protecting us from a bad choice or from continuing on the wrong path. Truly, the larger picture will emerge to show God's intimate and continuing care.

A GRACE FOR TODAY

Lord, help me follow your desires for me.

Is it you?

ISAIAH 45:6C–8, 18, 21C–25; LUKE 7:18B–23

And Jesus said to them in reply, "Go and tell John what you have seen and heard: the blind regain their sight, the lame walk, lepers are cleansed, the deaf hear, the dead are raised, the poor have the good news proclaimed to them." LUKE 7:22

In case we missed it, here it is again. Even John the Baptist needed to check and check again. Is Jesus the one whom Scripture promised? Is Jesus the one who is to come? Here, in Luke's telling of the story, John sends two disciples to ask, and Jesus sends them back with simple instructions: "Tell John what you have seen and heard."

That's it. Just tell John what you have seen. Just tell John what you have heard. There is no need to debate the issue. It is all about the good news: the blind see, the lame walk, the lepers are healed, the deaf hear, and even the dead are raised. These are no small feats for an itinerant preacher in Galilee two thousand years ago. Yet they happened, and more.

How difficult it is for us to believe. We have not seen, directly, what Jesus did. Neither have we heard, directly, the words of Jesus. But we know at a very deep level that these things have happened; these things did happen; these things are the very substance of our faith as Christians.

So how do we come up against this problem, which in large part is a problem of belief? Whom do we ask?

I think this is the problem of prayer. We are not in the situation where we can ship off two friends to the very presence of Jesus to ask him directly if it is really he whom we hear in prayer. Surely, we can be confused by what we hear when we pray. Sometimes we are confused because we hear nothing. Sometimes we are confused because we hear a lot. Which is it? Which comes from God?

The fact of the matter is our silent hearts can be invaded by false light. We can be perfectly at peace, with certainty and clarity, about one or another choice, and still be headed in the wrong direction.

Much has been written on this question. St. Ignatius explains in his Exercises the slippery turns of thought that can lead us astray. Sometimes we are certain, absolutely certain, of a decision, only to recognize much later it was wrong and that, as the phrase goes, "it seemed like a good idea at the time."

Sometimes we hear God in prayer, and we are correct. Sometimes we are not correct. I think a simple way to make the distinction is to listen to the words we use to describe how we think God has answered us. When God seems to be a nagging, dragging, punishing presence, we can safely assume it is not God. When God is a simple, calm, assuring presence, I think we can more safely assume the thoughts are from God.

After all, when asked, Jesus simply said to look to the evidence.

In any event, it is always a good idea to talk about prayer with another person, someone more experienced, someone a little farther along the road of prayer, someone who more often than not also has asked: "Are you the one?"

I am with you

ISAIAH 54:1–10; LUKE 7:24–30

Fear not, you shall not be put to shame; you need not blush,
for you shall not be disgraced....Though the mountains
leave their place and the hills be shaken, my love shall never
leave you nor my covenant of peace be shaken,
says the Lord, who has mercy on you. ISAIAH 54:4, 10

Christmas is getting closer. Suddenly, from out of the blue, we field an old accusation, an old argument, an old anger. There is a slight sense that something is not quite right, possibly with God. That seems to make no sense, as red ribbons spill joyfully at every turn, except inside churches still dark and wearing purple.

The church certainly practiced Advent as early as the fifth century, although Lent is known as early as the second century. (The old joke is that Lent was such a hit, they invented Advent.)

Strictly speaking, Advent is not a penitential season, but one of hopeful anticipation. Even so, it can be a time of deeper prayer and reflection, a time to take stock of ourselves and our relationships. Hence, many parishes offer penance services around this time in Advent. Some dioceses announce the simultaneous availability of confession in every parish.

It is important not to confuse the two seasons—Advent, one of hopeful longing for the birth of Christ, and Lent, one of purification and fasting prior to the Triduum of Holy Thursday, Good Friday, and Easter. Even so, the slowing down that comes with impending winter often brings us to face ourselves in ways that move us to contrition.

Here is where the words of Isaiah are at once startling and comforting. Here is what God directs and promises through the prophet, who speaks to our hearts as surely as he did to the people of God centuries ago. God's advice and promises: 1) do not fear; you will not be shamed; 2) do not be discouraged; you will not be disgraced; 4) no matter what, my love will endure; 5) my covenant of peace will remain.

I can really hate going to confession. I have awful confession stories of bored priests, of angry priests, of priests who just did not pay attention—not that long ago the priest's cell phone rang during my confession. I have learned to be selective when I place my heart before another person, especially a man I do not know. I think many people are the same. The tar-filled brush has colored our perceptions of men in ministry, and when the rattle outside matches personal experience, we simply walk away.

That can be a very smart thing to do. But there are good and holy priests still around who sit and listen carefully and non-judgmentally to what we have to say. And they have turned off their cell phones.

The last time I went to confession, I mentioned it to a friend who knows a lot about these things. "Did it work?" she softly asked.

You know, I think it did. That is the objective, after all. It is not about me alone, but about giving myself the chance to grow in hope and love, and to believe God's encouraging promise to be with me always.

A GRACE FOR TODAY

Lord, grant me the grace to accept your forgiving embrace.

We are all in this together

ISAIAH 56:1–3A, 6–8; JOHN 5:33–36

*Let not the foreigner say, when he would join himself to the
Lord, "The Lord will surely exclude me from his people." The
foreigners who join themselves to the Lord, ministering to him,
loving the name of the Lord and becoming his servants...
will be acceptable on my altar...For my house shall be called a
house of prayer for all peoples.* ISAIAH 56:3, 6-7

Every so often, Christmas is as late as it can be, on a Sunday,
so we get to hear these weekday readings for this Friday of the
Third Week of Advent. They cause us some pause. Christmas,
after all, belongs to all Christians, not one or another particular
church or denomination. Christmas is the feast nearly a third of
the world's population celebrates every year.

So why are there divisions within Christianity? Why are
there Catholics, Protestants, Orthodox, Anglicans? The list of
different churches and denominations is endless. The work of
ecumenical dialogue seems endless as well.

Yet today, Isaiah tells us that "foreigners" are acceptable in the
house of the Lord, because it is "a house of prayer for all peoples." We could extend the metaphor and begin thinking about
the other great Abrahamic religions—Judaism and Islam—and
the encouraging work done in interreligious dialogue among
and between them and Christian churches and denominations.
But for now, let us think about world Christianity.

How do we deal with "ecumenical dialogue" on the day-to-day level?

When I was in the seventh grade, I had to walk a little farther to get to my new school, a little over a mile away from home. There were a few ways I could walk along the winding roads in my development. One took me past a Protestant church. I always thought it was a Lutheran church, but now at least it seems to be an evangelical community church. I have some enduring memories of that place. First, there was never anyone around during the week. Second, the name of the preacher and his sermon topic were on the glass-enclosed blackboard with movable white letters. Third, they always had punch and cookies for the congregation on the front lawn after Sunday services.

The punch and cookies on the lawn really got to me.

Church in my grade-school days was a crowded auditorium affair, with screaming children, followed by parking-lot gridlock. People did not so much talk or even acknowledge each other before, during, or after Mass. We went and watched as the priest, assisted by desultory altar boys, went through the Mass in Latin, with his back turned most of the time. I do not know if they were facing east.

Quite quickly my view of "church" changed radically. The Second Vatican Council invited me in. Not completely, of course, but soon the Mass was something I was taking part in. I did not need to wait for bells to announce the consecration, because I could follow what was going on.

Of course, the Protestants and the Orthodox and the Anglicans had figured all that out years before. It was about language. It was about the vernacular. For me, it was about English.

One way we tend to separate ourselves is by language groups. I often wonder if Latin separated Catholics from the world and from each other. We were essentially strangers to each other because we literally did not pray together. And with no language of prayer to connect us, we remained disconnected after Mass. We seemed to be strangers sitting separately, attending a performance.

Perhaps in places I did not know about, and certainly in many Catholic churches now, there are punch and cookies on the lawn. In all our churches, we are sharing common culture and language. And more and more, "foreigners" are being recognized as fellow Christians searching for the One who is.

A GRACE FOR TODAY
Lord, grant me the grace to see you in all peoples.

Fiat!

Year A: Isaiah 7:10–14; Romans 1:1–7; Matthew 1:18–24
Year B: 2 Samuel 7:1–5, 8b–12, 14a, 16; Romans 16:25–27; Luke 1:26–38
Year C: Micah 5:1–4a; Hebrews 10:5–10; Luke 1:39–45

*"Do not be afraid, Mary, for you have found favor with God.
Behold, you will conceive in your womb and bear a son,
and you shall name him Jesus. He will be great and will be
called Son of the Most High, and the Lord God will give him
the throne of David his father, and he will rule over the house
of Jacob forever, and of his kingdom there will be no end."
But Mary said to the angel, "How can this be, since I have no
relations with a man?" And the angel said to her in reply,
"The Holy Spirit will come upon you, and the power of the Most
High will overshadow you. Therefore the child to be born will
be called holy, the Son of God. And behold, Elizabeth, your
relative, has also conceived a son in her old age, and this is
the sixth month for her who was called barren; for nothing
will be impossible for God." Mary said, "Behold, I am
the handmaid of the Lord. May it be done to me according
to your word." Then the angel departed from her.*

LUKE 1:30–38

Every gospel for the Fourth Sunday of Advent focuses on one
person: Mary, the mother of Jesus. Matthew recounts the annunciation, and Luke gives it more detail. The final gospel in
the church's three-year cycle follows the Lucan narrative and

tells of the visitation of Mary to Elizabeth, possibly to the hilltop town of Ein Karem southwest of Jerusalem.

By tradition, John the Baptist was born at Ein Karem, so it would make sense that Mary, on hearing her own news, would travel to John's mother, her cousin Elizabeth, to verify the added news that Elizabeth was also pregnant. Naysayers point out that Nazareth and Ein Karem are about ninety miles apart, but even walking slowly a woman could cover the distance in three or four days, and there is a tradition that Mary traveled by donkey.

And, on foot or donkey, why would she not want to go? The angel's announcement is quite precise and quite stunning. Mary, the simple woman—a girl, really—is to become the mother of the promised one, the savior of humanity, the Christ.

I walked up that hill once, to the place tradition says Mary met Elizabeth, to where they greeted each other and shared their news. It is a very steep climb, and when I made it I was much older than she. There is a sacredness to the place that words cannot box in. A feeling surrounds the place. It is the feeling, the sense, that so many other pilgrims, before, during, and after my own visit, were and would be consumed by the mystery of the Incarnation at that very spot.

Nothing, apparently, is impossible for God.

Atop the hill, the Franciscans keep a church at once feminine and strong. Above the church's entrance a mosaic of Mary traveling on a donkey oversees the courtyard where a modern statue of Mary meeting Elizabeth stands surrounded by more than forty ceramic tablets, each with the words of Mary's Magnificat in a different language of the world.

Inside, every detail speaks to Mary's experience and intuition, and to that of every woman. Underfoot, some of Mary's symbols—I recall the rose, a dove, a lily—appear in fine mosaic.

What is all this stone and plaster about? We can get very jaded at memorials and churches. We can say tradition needs a shaker-full of salt. We can say that none of this actually happened.

Or we can sit in peace with the first few joyful mysteries of the Rosary, with the Annunciation and the Visitation. We can choose to believe or not to believe that the angel of God asked Mary to participate fully in God's plan for her. We can believe or not believe that we are asked the same. She was terrified. So, often, are we as well. I think the consolation Mary offers is the fact that God's plans for us always work out, even if our own plans do not.

A GRACE FOR TODAY
Lord, grant me the grace to accept your invitations.

Friends and family

GENESIS 49:2, 8–10; MATTHEW 1:1–17

The book of the genealogy of Jesus Christ, the son of David,
the son of Abraham....Thus the total number of generations
from Abraham to David is fourteen generations; from David
to the Babylonian exile, fourteen generations; from
the Babylonian exile to the Christ, fourteen generations.

MATTHEW 1:1, 17

Today the church's preparation for Christmas intensifies. So does ours. Traffic crowds the roads; mail spills out of letterboxes; last-minute gifts come home to be wrapped after that one last office gathering. Once the tree is set up and the lights are strung, everything is set. Almost.

Today we begin to hear the "O antiphons," the phrases used to announce the gospel and the start of Vespers, or Evening Prayer. Each day, the church salutes a different attribute of Jesus, the One who is to come.

Today: "O Sapientia" (O Wisdom).

And where did he come from, this Wisdom?

Today, as every year on this day, we hear Jesus' family tree recited, all the way back to Abraham. There are so many generations that it seems possible that everyone in Jewish history is related to Jesus. In fact, the two books of Chronicles show almost four thousand years of ancestors to Jesus, whom we know was born over two thousand years ago and whose birth we celebrate in just a few days.

Who were all these people? Matthew gives them names, some familiar, some strange. He lists the people—the men—in Jesus' patrimony, beginning with Abraham. Christianity is just one of the "Abrahamic religions"—the principal others are Judaism and Islam—and more than half the world's population follows one of these three, or the six or seven smaller faiths that trace the same lineage.

So what is it about Abraham? In one of her poems, the late Carmelite Jessica Powers has a beautiful explanation of Abraham's response to God's call to leave his own country and travel on to a place God would show. Abraham never complained. He did not know how far he would have to travel. He did not know his fate. He just went.

So Powers compares her own responses to God's call: "I manipulate dates and decisions…take out old maps and stare." She punctures any inflated sense of righteousness or certainty she may have, and invites us to join her. We all have doubts. We all dither with appointments and commitments. We all fear closing out choices.

Powers brings out into the open what anyone who has made any permanent commitment fears: "Was there a call at all?" No matter when the iron gate shuts fast on other choices, every so often we hear its rusty scrape as one or another passing breeze attempts to dislodge the lock.

Somewhere in our own deep past, somewhere in the generations on generations that preceded and produced us, there is an Abraham who shared our fears and doubts and who is a part of the way we are. We can address our own ancestors, who crossed deserts or oceans to find their new lives; we can join in as Powers tells Abraham: ours "is a far and lonely journey, too."

We can also rest assured that whatever combination of ancestry and environment brought us to where we are today is part of God's plan for us. And, if we really stop to consider how much we are a part of our ancestors' deep history and their progeny, we might be able to see how very close we are to each and all around us.

A GRACE FOR TODAY

Lord, grant me the wisdom to see where I am going.

Parents

JEREMIAH 23:5–8; MATTHEW 1:18–25

*When his mother Mary was betrothed to Joseph, but before
they lived together, she was found with child through the Holy
Spirit. Joseph her husband, since he was a righteous man,
yet unwilling to expose her to shame, decided to divorce her
quietly. Such was his intention when, behold, the angel of
the Lord appeared to him in a dream and said, "Joseph, son
of David, do not be afraid to take Mary your wife into your
home. For it is through the Holy Spirit that this child has been
conceived in her. She will bear a son and you are to name him
Jesus, because he will save his people from their sins."...When
Joseph awoke, he did as the angel of the Lord had commanded
him and took his wife into his home.* MATTHEW 1:18-21, 24-25*

Matthew in today's gospel focuses on dear Joseph, who, like
Mary, was asked to accept the improbable and do the impossible. She would be the mother of God. He would accept his
pregnant fiancée without question.

Or would he? There are many stunning works of art that de-
pict the annunciation. Botticelli, da Vinci, Caravaggio, Titian...
an endless list of greats and others put their talents at the dis-
posal of this most amazing story. The angel—we know him
as Gabriel—comes to Mary and, in the art, wordlessly brings
her the news. We wonder, as we watch the static scene, how we
might react.

There are fewer depictions of Joseph's encounter with the angel. Even so, Francisco Goya's eighteenth-century rendering of this gospel passage absorbs the power of the moment. Think of it. Here is poor Joseph, a simple man faced with this message from this angel: your fiancée will bear the Messiah.

Joseph was not a politician or a merchant. He was not a teacher or a landowner. He was a craftsman—tradition calls him a carpenter—and he likely went to ply his trade each day in the ancient city of Sepphoris, just a few miles from Nazareth. He has found a prospective bride, and she has accepted him.

But then everything changes. What is poor Joseph to do? He could break their promised troth. But then there is the dream, and when he awakes this simple man decides to keep his promise to Mary. He decides to raise her child as his own.

Now, they are both committed. She will have the Child; he will raise the Son. Joseph is charged with protecting both.

One the one hand, it makes no sense. Babies don't appear out of thin air. Joseph and Mary, the conventional wisdom complains, had to have conceived Jesus the old fashioned way. That would have been on Joseph's mind and Mary's just as well. I know myself I have quite often questioned this part of the story.

I always end up looking at it this way: God can do whatever God wants. If I believe that Jesus is the Christ, the Son of God, the Third Person of the Blessed Trinity, then why would I have an ounce of doubt about his patrimony or his birth? No matter how it came about in fact, in fact it came about. And I am perfectly happy to accept the story as it has been told for thousands of years, and to know Mary and Joseph as parents to the Christ.

We have already heard the reading—it too often seems endless in Sunday Mass—of Jesus' direct ancestors. Now we get a close-up of a tender father torn between belief and unbelief. How like us all, even today.

A GRACE FOR TODAY

Lord, help me learn more about gentle Joseph.

Listening

JUDGES 13:2–7, 24–25A; LUKE 1:5–25

*Then, when the whole assembly of the people was praying
outside at the hour of the incense offering, the angel of the Lord
appeared to him, standing at the right of the altar of incense.
Zechariah was troubled by what he saw, and fear came upon
him. But the angel said to him, "Do not be afraid, Zechariah,
because your prayer has been heard. Your wife Elizabeth will
bear you a son, and you shall name him John. And you will have
joy and gladness, and many will rejoice at his birth, for he will
be great in the sight of the Lord."* LUKE 1:10-15

Politicians have "advance people" who prepare things before
they go to a given town. They make sure all the announcements
are out, that everybody knows who will come and what will
happen. Today's Scriptures have a couple of "advance angels."
Here, two angels foretell two births: first, that of Samson, the
strong man of the Israelites, and next, that of John the Baptist,
the itinerant preacher who in turn announced the coming of
Christ.

I have always liked Gabriel, the angel who spoke to Mary
and who told Zechariah he would have a son. Many years ago I
received a postcard from a friend who worked in broadcasting
in New York. I think I had just published an article or a book.
One side of the card reproduced a detail of a beautiful painting,

focusing on Gabriel at the annunciation. On the other side, my friend wrote, "greetings, from one announcer to another." I like that. Of course, his clever turn of phrase went in both of our directions. He worked in front of a camera; I worked in front of a computer.

I like his greeting and its implication not only for myself but for every other messenger of the gospel. What, after all, are we doing besides passing along the message? And what else are we doing besides waiting for the message to come to us? And are we listening?

Sometimes when I hear of Gabriel's annunciation to Mary or even here, as he speaks to Zechariah, I burrow in my mind to places where I believe the Lord has asked me to do one thing or another. When was I sure? When I was absolutely clear of one choice or another? When did I know God's word helped form a decision within my heart?

That wondering can be, as well, an invitation to miss the point. We listen and we speak. What if I put on Gabriel's shoes—or wings—and think of what I might announce?

St. Francis of Assisi is often quoted: "Preach the gospel at all times. Use words if necessary." The Franciscans were not noted as preachers—that was the charism St. Dominic brought to the church at a time when only bishops could preach formally—and there is no documentation crediting the phrase to Francis.

Even so, Francis may have given that advice, that succinct pointer to the intimate relationship between words and actions. In the thirteenth-century Franciscan Rule, we find this: "All the friars...should preach by their deeds." Francis sends us all in a very good direction. He certainly speaks to me. My business is words, but I live in the world. My words make no sense if they do not echo what I do and how I am.

I think the task of life is to be who we are asked to be. That begins with listening. That deepens with hearing. That finds fruition with acting.

So we listen and we preach. Sometimes we will be quite surprised at what we hear. Poor Zechariah was struck dumb when he heard what Gabriel had to say, when he learned he would have a son. We too may be "dumbstruck" when we finally recognize God's plan for us, especially about the preaching part.

A GRACE FOR TODAY

Lord, grant me the grace to be your voice.

Saying yes

Isaiah 7:10–14; Luke 1:26–38

"Behold, you will conceive in your womb and bear a son,
and you shall name him Jesus.
He will be great and will be called Son of the Most High,
and the Lord God will give him the throne of David his father,
and he will rule over the house of Jacob forever,
and of his Kingdom there will be no end."
Mary said, "Behold, I am the handmaid of the Lord.
May it be done to me according to your word."
Then the angel departed from her. LUKE 1:31-33, 38

There is nothing ordinary about the annunciation. Mary is visited by the angel Gabriel, who says she will become the mother of the promised one—today's antiphon sings of the "Key of David." Extraordinary as it is, the birth of Christ depends on human acts. Mary must agree. Eventually, Joseph will agree. And the Child will be born.

Mary did say "yes" to Gabriel's announcement that she would be the mother of God, but not before asking the obvious question: how?

Wouldn't you?

I'm not a fan of bad spiritual direction—the kind where the director talks all the time and provides all the answers— but I do believe in the deep value of sitting with someone both trained and able to listen, to talk about what God seems to ask.

There is no getting around it. God does "ask" us things in various ways. We can rattle off lists: God asks me to be kind to my family and community; God asks me to work hard every day; God asks me to take care of my health; and so it goes.

The lists are nice, but I think the most basic thing God asks of us is to be who we are. That's all. That is not insignificant, but it is really all God asks of us. I think if we pay attention to that single request, everything else falls into place.

So how do we find out who we are supposed to be? I would think the first step would be finding out who we are right now. We were born in a certain place and time; we have certain talents and desires; we have friends and family, neighbors and coworkers. Most times, we are pretty much on the road to who we are supposed to be, mainly because we paid attention to what happened as we grew up, as we went to school, as we took first jobs and first steps toward a permanent personal commitment.

But the question still appears. Who am I supposed to be?

It never goes away.

Ignatian spirituality includes the concept of the "Magis"—related to the Jesuit motto, ad majorem Dei gloriam (to the greater glory of God)—and I think this single word urges us forward, to the more, the better, all in God's service. Magis is a word I cannot say without opening my arms wide to embrace… what? I think my embrace is of what God asks, and I think what God asks, first, is for me to love.

So, as I think Mary did, I try to open my heart and my arms to God's desires for me. I cannot do it alone. The choices life spreads before me and you include many goods. But we have limited lives, limited days to joyfully accept God's gifts. So, while the wide-open acceptance of what God puts before me sounds all hunky-dory, the fact is, like the rest of the world, I need to make choices.

Back to spiritual direction. Here I can safely talk about what I think I hear, notice, and feel about God's desires for me. Here I am looking in my own life for the kind of openness Mary showed and shows us over and over. Here I am trying to distinguish what comes from God, what comes from myself, and what comes from the negative force or forces in my life, these last aimed at attacking my very human nature.

I know the Spirit of the Lord will come upon me. I know as well I must cooperate. I must, however, cooperate in God's plan for me to become and be who God intends. For me, and for all of us, once we say "yes," the rest is easy.

A GRACE FOR TODAY

Lord, grant me the grace to make my "yes" complete.

Secrets of the dark

SONG OF SONGS 2:8–14; LUKE 1:39–45

When Elizabeth heard Mary's greeting, the infant leaped in her
womb, and Elizabeth, filled with the Holy Spirit, cried out in a
loud voice and said, "Most blessed are you among women, and
blessed is the fruit of your womb. And how does this happen to
me, that the mother of my Lord should come to me? For at the
moment the sound of your greeting reached my ears, the infant
in my womb leaped for joy. Blessed are you who believed that
what was spoken to you by the Lord would be fulfilled."

LUKE 1:41–45

We can talk all we want to friends, relatives, colleagues, psycholo-
gists, and spiritual directors, but the bottom line is: God comes to
us in secret. There is no getting away from it. When we are really
interested in what the Lord has in mind for us, we need to sit,
quietly, alone, peacefully, silently, talking to God, yes, but most of
all listening. That is what Mary did. She listened.

Today's readings celebrate the listening heart. The writer of
the Song of Songs says God is "like a gazelle or a young stag...
leaping across the hills"—the graceful lover who sparks in me
that feeling of joy, of happiness, at his appearance.

I think we can get a glimpse of that joy and happiness as we
consider Mary coming to Elizabeth at Ein Karem. Elizabeth
knows immediately what has happened to Mary, and she is
filled with happiness. Elizabeth tells Mary: "the moment the

sound of your greeting reached my ears, the infant in my womb leaped for joy."

Sometimes I think I need a refresher course in "Feelings 101."

So what is this "joy"?

Not long before Christmas one year, I visited an old convent, a large building with many corridors and turns. At one point, instead of making a right to get back to where I came from, I went straight ahead and ended up in the chapel. There appeared before me, suddenly and unexpectedly, a Christmas tree filled with bright, white lights. I actually drew in a quick breath, held my hands together beneath my chin, and said, rather out loud, "Oh, my."

That was joy. It was a joy mixed with gratitude for the unexpected, for the beautiful, for the celebration to come, for the fact of where I was at that very moment.

It is good to remember that feeling.

Today is the darkest day of the year. The antiphon sings of the dayspring—the dawn—about to come. We may not be bouncing with joy and gratitude, perhaps because prayer has gotten dull, or illness is upon us, or any of the other turns that life can take have brought us where we did not expect to go.

As with anything else, the task is just to keep on keeping on. The earth still slumbers, waiting for the coming of the Messiah. We may sit, waiting, hoping, for a visit to engulf us in silent joy. No matter who else shows up these days, I think we can rest assured that the Lord will come, quietly and in secret, and we will be able to rest in that joy.

A GRACE FOR TODAY
Lord, help me sit joyfully with you.

Thank you!

1 SAMUEL 1:24–28; LUKE 1:46–56

"My soul proclaims the greatness of the Lord;
my spirit rejoices in God my savior,
for he has looked upon his lowly servant.
From this day all generations will call me blessed:
the Almighty has done great things for me,
and holy is his Name.
He has mercy on those who fear him
in every generation.
He has shown the strength of his arm,
and has scattered the proud in their conceit.
He has cast down the mighty from their thrones
and has lifted up the lowly.
He has filled the hungry with good things,
and the rich he has sent away empty.
He has come to the help of his servant Israel
for he remembered his promise of mercy,
the promise he made to our fathers,
to Abraham and his children forever." LUKE 1:46-55

Years ago, I believe in the mid-1970s, John Michael Talbot recorded his version of Mary's Magnificat. His is a hauntingly simple rendition of the prayer we hear today.

For many years, when I lived in Manhattan, in the evening after supper, I would pop in a little blue cassette and listen as

Talbot sang "My soul proclaims the greatness of the Lord."

That is what I was trying to do. That is all any of us tries to do.

Now I can bring Talbot's music up on YouTube, or just let it play along in my head as I read the Magnificat. It is, to me at least, a powerful reminder of Mary's gratitude for her life. It helps me be grateful for my own.

Of course, gratitude is the cornerstone of the spiritual life. It is as well the cornerstone of a productive and happy life. I was asked once to consult on a project on what is called "positive psychology" at the University of Pennsylvania, and while there I was asked to present on the Ignatian Examen, the short prayer many people make once or twice a day.

There are many ways to do the Examen. Traditionally, there are five steps: 1) become aware of the presence of God; 2) gratefully review the day; 3) pay attention to your emotions; 4) choose one event or feature of the day and pray with it; 5) look toward tomorrow. I think there is a simple way of working with these steps: Where did I love? Where was I loved? Where can I love?

The key here is gratitude, and that is what I told the Ph.D. students in psychology at the University of Pennsylvania.

Positive psychology has many "gratitude" practices. One, like the Examen, is performed before bed. You are asked to find three good things in the day and to be grateful for them. When I explained the Ignatian Examen, one of the professors who essentially invented positive psychology was in the room. He said: "That's my stuff!"

Well, not exactly. St. Ignatius lived four and a half centuries ago. I think Ignatius had a handle on some pretty good psychology himself. The difference is that Ignatius teaches us, first, to be grateful to God. Hence, we offer and return in gratitude all we have been given, day in, day out.

We see this in today's readings. Hannah was delighted with her son, Samuel, and offered him to the Lord. Mary praised God in gratitude with her Magnificat. Today's antiphon praises the "King of All Nations," the Christ who is to come.

The onslaught of holiday chores and cares may cancel any thoughts of singing, but the lowering fog of too much to do should not let any of us forget to say "thank you" to God, to others, and to ourselves. Life itself is such a magnificent gift.

A GRACE FOR TODAY

Lord, grant me the grace to be grateful.

Messages and messengers

MALACHI 3:1–4, 23–24; LUKE 1:57–66

Thus says the Lord God: Lo, I am sending my messenger
to prepare the way before me; and suddenly
there will come to the temple the Lord whom you seek, and the
messenger of the covenant whom you desire.
Yes, he is coming, says the Lord of hosts. MALACHI 3:1

An interesting thing about the Book of Malachi is that the name
Malachi is a transliteration of the Hebrew *ykalm,* "my messen-
ger"—the messenger of Yahweh. So who is God's messenger? Is it
John the Baptist? Is it Jesus? Is it you? Who sends? Who receives?

For some people, this season, the messages never end.
Mailboxes are stuffed with cards. Telephone messages and e-mails
never end. Parcels and packages pile up on the stoop. You see the
delivery folks and mail carriers scurry along in the neighborhood,
and you come home every day to greetings from far and wide.

These days, I tend to think of the folks who come home to
nothing. I tend to think of the people who sit watching out the
window for the mail carrier, who more often than not passes by
without leaving anything. This may be happening to you.

Christmas can be a rough season. Today promises not only
Jesus but John. We need them both. We need John to tell us,
again and again, that the one coming is Jesus, the Christ. We
need to know that Jesus will come, has come, and lives among
us. But we all need a closer touch from the human "Jesus" in our

lives. We need people—the Christs among us—to tell us we are remembered this season, especially this week. We need to know we are loved.

I happen to be a greeting card fan. I send cards for all sorts of reasons—Christmas, certainly, but then there is Valentine's Day, Saint Patrick's Day, Easter, Mother's Day, Father's Day, birthdays, and best of all, Thanksgiving. My writing habits will not alone support the national greeting card industry, but I do send a lot of cards. I think I know a lot of people who do not get cards or gifts at Christmas or for their birthdays. I may not know them very well, but why not send a card?

Postage and greeting cards now cost ten times what they did when I would come home from school each December day to help my mother with her cards. She was a teacher and had worked in a few different schools. Everybody got a card—season's greetings for non-Christians—and everybody got a hand-written note, a word of cheer. She wasn't running for Congress, she was just nice. I was in charge of addresses and stamps.

It was a lot of work, but the older I get, the more I understand it. For too many people, there is no frenzy of contact with family, community, and colleagues these last few days before Christmas. So the days can be very long and lonely for them, just as they can be long and lonely for us.

Of course, it goes both ways. Sometimes we are so entrapped in our own sadness we do not move to extend greetings to someone else. I think that is a huge mistake. I think you get cheer by giving it. I also think we are all messengers of the Christ who is and who is to come.

Lord, let me be your messenger.

Blessed!

2 Samuel 7:1–5, 8b–12, 14a, 16; Luke 1:67–79

"Blessed be the Lord, the God of Israel;
for he has come to his people and set them free.
He has raised up for us a mighty Savior,
born of the house of his servant David...
You, my child, shall be called the prophet of the Most High,
for you will go before the Lord to prepare his way,
to give his people knowledge of salvation
by the forgiveness of their sins.
In the tender compassion of our God
the dawn from on high shall break upon us,
to shine on those who dwell in darkness
and the shadow of death,
and to guide our feet into the way of peace."

LUKE 1:68–69, 76–79

Many folks skip morning Mass on Christmas Eve day, planning to go to the afternoon vigil Mass—often the family Mass that includes a children's pageant—or the later "Midnight Mass," which may more likely be celebrated in the early evening.

The pity of missing the morning Mass is that you do not hear the Benedictus, Zechariah's song of praise at the circumcision of his son, John the Baptist, proclaimed as the gospel. It is a spectacular prayer.

Many people who have the opportunity to celebrate Lauds,

or Morning Prayer, can probably recite this canticle by heart because it is said or sung every morning. They say it was introduced to Lauds by St. Benedict, a patron saint of Europe and founder of western monasticism. So nearly every day the church has the opportunity to sing God's praise along with Zechariah. The canticle is a beautiful song of gratitude that I think recognizes, even reinforces, the comforting care the Lord gives each one of us.

The daily challenge is to believe what the Benedictus proclaims. Christmas is the day when we can truly use Zechariah's words to proclaim our own belief and joy in the Christ now born to save us. The list of things we hear as God's promises is amazing: forgiveness of sins; the tender compassion of God; guidance into the way of peace.

Whether we made it to morning Mass or not today, we can sit in somewhat exhausted solitude and ponder these promises. Our sins will be forgiven; we will know the tender compassion of God; we will be guided into the way of peace.

I like to remind myself that the next time I think I never sin, I should check in with my best friend. The more we progress in the life of Christ—what folks like to call the spiritual life—the more refined our faults and failings become. Nothing like the person we are closest to to help us look in the mirror.

Sin, genuine sin, always begins with the little things, the little choices. Often it begins with what my graduate professor called "thought crime." You float a negative thought about someone. Soon it turns to a comment. Next thing you know, it becomes an action. So suddenly you ostracize the one you secretly criticized. Others may join you. It's not healthy. It's not good.

So we seek the tender compassion of God. Each evening, as I lay out the graces of the day in gratitude, I look into my own heart to see where and how I loved—God, others, and myself. Some people teach that the Examen is time to see how we "co-labored" with Christ, but that to me speaks too much of workplace review, and it can quickly become accusatory: I did not work hard enough; I did not do this or that.

Of course, we will find in our day things we might have softened, might have done a little differently. But what we look for is what we have been promised: the tender compassion of God. That soothes the ache when we see mistakes and gives us hope for the morrow. It also helps us to be grateful for what we have been given, for what we have, for all we are.

The practice of reviewing our lives in God will guide us into the way of peace. And it is the Prince of Peace whom we are celebrating.

A GRACE FOR TODAY

Lord, grant me the grace to know myself as blessed.

Let there be light!

ISAIAH 62:1–5; ACTS 13:16–17, 22–25; MATTHEW 1:1–25

For the Lord delights in you.   ISAIAH 62:4

The Christmas Vigil Mass is often celebrated in parishes as the children's Mass and pageant. The little ones line up: the shepherds and angels, Mary and Joseph, the innkeeper, the three wise men. There are a few camels and sheep around, and a bright star hangs over the scene, whether in the church or in the auditorium.

I often recall the story of the young boy, all prepped for his one big line as the innkeeper. Joseph and Mary appear at the door, perhaps worse from the wear of their long journey. The innkeeper has been practicing all week. He stands ready, behind the barred door of the inn. The knock comes. He opens the door. Warmth surrounds the travelers and bright light shines out. Joseph says plaintively, "My wife is with child, about to give birth, and we have nowhere to stay." The innkeeper says, "Aw, c'mon in."

Of course the audience cracks up at this new take on the story of the birth of Jesus. The idea of Mary and Joseph settling in to a comfortable Bethlehem B&B, rather than down in the barn below, is too much for the heart. The rest of the cast is hopelessly confused.

Somehow the pageant gets rescued. Jesus is born—in the stable—and the sheep and camels and angels and Magi get their time onstage. The curtains close, and the Mass begins.

You have to love it. No matter how many times the children of the parish put on their shepherd's robes, their halos, their wings, and all the rest, the story of Jesus coming simply and quietly in the most humble of circumstances is rather delightful. As the Mass progresses, above a baby's wail—no doubt the cry of a brother or sister of one of the star actors this afternoon or evening—we may hear the promise of Isaiah enfolding us and the children: "For the Lord delights in you."

God does. God really does. God delights in them and in you as a precious creation destined to live and love in light and grace.

This Christmas Eve, the lights are shining in the church and in our hearts, even as outside entire nations may lumber about in the dark, making huge decisions that negatively affect everyone on the planet. The challenge to us, this evening, this night, and every day of Christmastide is to recall with family and friends that Jesus comes with the light of justice and peace for all. We are called and challenged to know God's love for ourselves and to share that love with family, with friends, with neighbors, with entire communities. We are called and challenged to open our hearts and arms in love.

Come to think of it, that young innkeeper showed the real meaning of Christmas.

A GRACE FOR TODAY

Lord, grant me a welcoming heart.

Celebrate life!

Mass during the Night: ISAIAH 9:1–6; TITUS 2:11–14; LUKE 2:1–14

Mass at Dawn: ISAIAH 62:11–12; TITUS 3:4–7; LUKE 2:15–20

Mass During the Day: ISAIAH 52:7–10; HEBREWS 1:1–6; JOHN 1:1–18

Now there were shepherds in that region living in the fields and keeping the night watch over their flock. The angel of the Lord appeared to them and the glory of the Lord shone around them, and they were struck with great fear. The angel said to them, "Do not be afraid; for behold, I proclaim to you good news of great joy that will be for all the people. For today in the city of David a savior has been born for you who is Christ and Lord."

LUKE 2:8–11

If you were present in first-century Palestine, the people you would be least likely to associate with were the shepherds. They were lower than low-class. They lived in the fields with their animals. I am not sure we can appreciate their simplicity.

I have seen the place called Shepherds' Field, near Bethlehem. It is a sacred place high above the village and rather barren, now cared for by Franciscans. There is not much to see, except the fields and the horizon. I cannot imagine spending my life there, simply tending sheep. For the shepherds it was surely a very difficult and simple life.

When Pope Francis talks about pastors having the "smell of their sheep," I think that simplicity and dedication is what he is talking about. The shepherds were close to the flock; they never left it. And they were uncomplicated people.

I think when you think about it, Christ was pretty uncomplicated too. He spoke plainly. He spoke simply. If what we have are not his exact words, it matters not. We know for sure that he came in the most humble way to the simplest of people.

The point? I think the point is that Christ was—and is—available to every single one of us.

So it is Christmas! The bells are ringing and the church is filled with light. The candles glow, the tree lights shine, the wreaths wear red bows, and everybody says, "Merry Christmas" as genuine joy fills the air. And what is the message? The three Masses for Christmas day each include readings from Isaiah, the prophet of hope.

Now hope has arrived in the person of Jesus!

What do we hope for? In the developed world, Christmas marks the culmination of a grand shopping season. The rushing and buying and wrapping and hiding of gifts large and small has ended with a smaller or larger bang, depending on how many children are around. Underneath the generosity of material giving are the deeper gifts of family, friends, and community, no matter the financial circumstances. Many simple hopes are fulfilled.

But we might know sadness this day. The many Christmases past may dance about our memories as better than this Christmas in one way or another. That can be because we may not have gifts, or special friends, or even someone with whom to share a Christmas dinner. Things are just not like they used to be. No matter what today is, or what it may bring, it will never be the same as before.

There can be ways to turn that sadness around. It has become almost trite to tell people to "live in the present," but, after all, that is all we have. The past is gone, only to remain in the vaults of memory; the future is not here, only in waiting. Neither past nor future should trouble us terribly this day. We can be grateful for the memories of happy Christmases past; we can look forward in gratitude to a promised lunch or dinner. But the bottom line is that we are here, now, today, this minute, with whomever, wherever; and we have been given this time to share, even if we are alone.

When I am alone unexpectedly, I tend to ask the Lord why he needs to spend so much time with me. And when you come to think about it, we are all alone in one way or another. So, like the lonely shepherds, maybe this day it would be good to stare in wonder at the star, at the gifts of nature around you, the sounds, sights, weather and, most of all, people—people you know and people you do not know—who echo the earth's excitement about the coming of Jesus in hope.

Jesus the Christ has come into the world and lives in our hearts. That is the simple hope that Christmas brings.

A GRACE FOR TODAY
Lord, grant me the grace to accept your gift of hope.

**CHRISTMAS IS A MOVABLE FEAST,
SO FOLLOW THE DAYS AS THEY
UNFOLD THIS YEAR.**

Beware!

ACTS 6:8–10; 7:54–59; MATTHEW 10:17–22

Jesus said to his disciples: "Beware of men,
for they will hand you over to courts and scourge you
in their synagogues, and you will be led before governors
and kings for my sake as a witness before them and the pagans.
You will be hated by all because of my name, but whoever
endures to the end will be saved."

MATTHEW 10:17–18, 22

The day after Christmas offers a comeuppance for all of us. In today's readings, the angels have flown away, the shepherds are back with their flocks, and although the church is still hung with wreaths, already we are learning about the cost of discipleship. Christianity is no walk in the park.

Saint Stephen, remembered today as the first martyr, is one of seven named as chosen by the community to do what we now call diaconal work. Once he and six others were put forth , the apostles laid hands on them and set them to do the works of service we now associate with the diaconate.

Stephen was apparently quite the debater. He got himself into trouble by saying God did not live in a place "made by human hands," that is, in the Temple. While his objective was to argue that Jesus was the Christ and Lord, his words made it sound as if the Jewish authorities were idolaters, that they worshiped idols. Tried and found guilty by the Sanhedrin, Stephen was stoned to death in the presence of Saul of Tarsus, whom we now know as St. Paul.

If you think about it, there is a sobering coda to Stephen's story in the world today. In many places people are killed—stoned, beheaded, burned to death—simply for being Christian. They are not deacons or bishops. They are not orators or teachers. They are simple Christians, in many cases people no more complicated than the shepherds who followed the star to the place where Jesus was born. Like Stephen, they are killed just for professing Christianity, for believing in Jesus as the Christ, for following Jesus as King and Lord.

In less dramatic ways we are all like Stephen, challenged by our own Sanhedrins of lust, gluttony, greed, sloth, wrath, envy, and pride to deny Christ. These capital vices and their relations can lead us in larger or smaller ways to deny Christ and turn us to an idol "made from human hands."

Years ago I had a repeated and ongoing discussion with a professor friend of mine, a Jesuit priest philosopher named Quentin Lauer. At some point during a shared meal, one of us would ask: What would you do if someone held a gun to your head and said if you denied Christ, he would not kill you?

Think about it.

What would you say?

We always came up with the same response. Anyone hateful enough to threaten to kill you is probably a liar. So, his word is no good. Therefore, once you deny Christ, he kills you.

Then where are you?

I think we can see the honor and courage of the new martyrs of Christianity, the Stephens of Somalia and Iraq and Syria beheaded, knifed, burned simply for being Christians and refusing to deny it.

That we in civilized nations at peace or relatively so do not fear the choice with a gun to our heads or a sword at our necks can move us to a complacency about what it means to be—and remain—Christian. The little choices mark us as Christians every day. The small, often silent choices to return the overpayment, to live quietly and justly, to pay attention to political issues, and to make our voices heard can be risky and endanger not so much our physical lives but the ways in which our precious lives unfold in relation to a world quite often very hostile to Christianity.

A GRACE FOR TODAY
Lord, grant me the grace to profess my belief in you.

Deference

1 John 1:1–4; John 20:1a, 2–8

On the first day of the week, Mary Magdalene ran and went to Simon Peter and to the other disciple whom Jesus loved, and told them, "They have taken the Lord from the tomb, and we do not know where they put him."...The other disciple ran faster than Peter and arrived at the tomb first; he bent down and saw the burial cloths there, but did not go in. When Simon Peter arrived after him, he went into the tomb.... Then the other disciple also went in, the one who had arrived at the tomb first, and he saw and believed.

JOHN 20:1A, 2–6, 8

The scholarship can make you dizzy. As much as I would like to argue that Mary Magdalene is the beloved disciple, let's take the usual interpretations of this gospel at face value and say it is John. Today is John's feast, and the gospel story shows two things: his deference to Peter's seniority, and his deference to Peter's authority.

We must recall that the apostles, excepting Peter, may have been quite young—even teenagers—when they began to follow Jesus. In Matthew 17:24–27, only Jesus and Peter seem to have paid the temple tax. That would indicate two things: that Jesus and Peter were relative contemporaries, and that the others were under the age of twenty and therefore did not have to pay the tax. So Peter, even if not Jesus' exact age, would have been older than the other apostles. We know as well from other passages that Jesus selected Peter as "the rock" upon which he would build his church.

Can you picture the scene here? John, somewhat younger than Peter, races ahead to the tomb on hearing Mary Magdalene's news: "They have taken the Lord from the tomb, and we do not know where they put him." John, perhaps ten or twelve years younger than Peter, arrives there first. He does look in, but he waits for Peter to arrive and lets him enter first.

When you think of it, it is a sweet scene and a very kind story. In many ways, it is repeated every day. The students let me on the bus first this afternoon. The young person at the checkout counter was patient as you fished for coins the other day. A younger niece or nephew brought dinners for their ailing aunt for the entire month.

Deference to age is a good and common courtesy. Deference to authority becomes a bit more difficult. Ironically, it gets increasingly difficult to grant that deference as we age.

Then it gets very easy. I do not know at what age we decide we know more than the one in charge and that we have a better view of things. I do not know exactly when we assert that we can make all decisions on our own, and ignore authority. But at some point after that, we truly grow up to recognize that authority—and obedience—are (or at least can be) very positive.

Of course there are many types and levels of authority. We know enough at any age not to ignore traffic signs and signals. It is not a very bright enterprise to drive the wrong way down a one-way street. But there are other signs and signals we tend to ignore, and sometimes we are quite foolhardy and go racing the wrong way down a metaphorical one-way street of our own accord.

When I bring the concept back to the everyday, I notice even now the struggle not to criticize the one "in charge." In fact, I think everyone can admit that failing. The big things we know about. The small ones eat away at the enamel: "Well, she may be in charge, but I would have done it this way…" And the small ones can make all the difference.

A GRACE FOR TODAY

Lord, grant me the grace of deference.

Loss and grief

1 John 1:5—2:2; Matthew 2:13–18

*Then was fulfilled what had been said through Jeremiah
the prophet: A voice was heard in Ramah, sobbing and loud
lamentation; Rachel weeping for her children, and she would
not be consoled, since they were no more.* **MATTHEW 2:17-18**

The Scriptures recount a terrible story today, the Feast of the
Holy Innocents. Herod, the ambitious Roman client king
of Judea, sent the Magi to Bethlehem to find the newborn
Messiah. He directed them to come back and tell him where the
child was, so he could worship him.

The Magi were having none of it. They returned by another
route, bypassing Herod. Enraged by their action and intimidat-
ed by news of the birth of a king, Herod ordered the slaughter
of all the boys under the age of two in Bethlehem.

Meanwhile, Joseph, warned in a dream, had already taken
Mary and Jesus to Egypt. The child Jesus was safe, but the others!

Can you imagine? How many children perished in the
slaughter? How many mothers lost their dreams, crushed
by Herod's cruelty? The writer of Matthew's gospel quotes
Jeremiah: *"A voice was heard in Ramah, sobbing and loud lamentation; Rachel weeping for her children, and she would not be consoled, since they were no more."*

Bethlehem was a small village. Some scholars estimate as few
as twenty children slaughtered because of Herod's insecurities.

Whether twenty or two thousand, there is nothing quite so sad as the image of a dead or dying child.

We see them all the time, so often we might nearly be immune to feeling. Newspapers, television, and Facebook alike show starving children in the poorest nations, young failed emigrants drowned on foreign shores, dead babies atop piles of trash. Some statisticians say 21,000 children die around the world each day.

I wonder if we can ever appreciate the deep suffering in this world, now, as well as at the time of Jesus. I do not think anyone besides the mother can fully understand the grief a dead child brings. In Genesis we learn that Rachel died in childbirth on her way to Bethlehem. She was buried at Ramah. In Jeremiah, Rachel "weeps" again as her children are led into captivity from there. Here, in Matthew, we can imagine mothers and fathers weeping uncontrollably at Herod's heinous act.

No matter how many times we hear stories such as these, they are easy to miss. When I was in fourth grade after-school religious education classes, we took turns reading Bible stories aloud. I was called upon to read the story of today's gospel from my slim, yellow, hard-bound book—I think the first hardbound book I ever owned. I stood, and proudly proclaimed the story of the "holy incidents."

Some classmates laughed, and I was quite embarrassed. I managed to get through the rest of the reading because of the way my teacher, Sister Thomas Aquinas, OP, reacted. Perhaps my most cherished school memory is of the kindly way she softly corrected me. I don't think I ever feared embarrassment again, although I have never forgotten the "holy incidents."

I think we tend to build emotional barriers to loss, embarrassment, and grief. I am not sure that is terribly healthy. Rachel wept at her first loss, wept again at the loss for the Jewish people, and now weeps a third time as the male toddlers of Bethlehem are killed by the order of a neurotic, self-centered ruler. I think it good to weep with her.

I stumble over words sometimes, and when I do I hear the gentle words of Sister Thomas Aquinas. I think it good to accept her encouragement.

I read about dead babies every day, and with their mothers I weep in rage at the stupidities of war, famine, and fate. I think it good to feel their grief.

A GRACE FOR TODAY
Lord, grant me the grace of empathy.

Obedience

Year A: Sirach 3:2–6, 12–14; Colossians 3:12–21;
Matthew 2:13–15, 19–23
Year B: Genesis 15:1–6, 21:1–3; Hebrews 11:8, 11–12, 17–19;
Luke 2:22–40
Year C: 1 Samuel 1:20–22, 24–28; 1 John 3:1–2, 21–24;
Luke 2:41–52

Thinking that he was in the caravan, they journeyed for a day
and looked for him among their relatives and acquaintances,
but not finding him, they returned to Jerusalem to look for him.
After three days they found him in the temple,
sitting in the midst of the teachers...and his mother said to him,
"Son, why have you done this to us? Your father and I
have been looking for you with great anxiety."
And he said to them, "Why were you looking for me?
Did you not know that I must be in my Father's house?"

LUKE 2:44–46, 48–49

The readings for Holy Family Sunday offer a wide variety of choices. They all have to do with family, and they all have to do with obedience.

Many people mistake the concept of obedience, often deriding the military in so doing. Not long ago, I heard a woman relate unapprovingly the details of a televised documentary about naval training in her country. She particularly decried the fact that if clothing was found incorrectly folded during inspections in living quarters, the task had to be redone. She gave a few other examples about the demanding attention to detail required in military and naval training. All I could think was, I hope she appreciates the fact that the pilot on her next plane ride was trained that way, whether inside or outside national service. Naval and military personnel are trained to be absolutely certain about the details. They are trained to be obedient to the details.

That sort of obedience becomes habitual, and it is routinely necessary in many walks of life. Not only pilots but dentists, surgeons, surveyors, architects, and hundreds of other professionals must be exact and precise in what they do.

So, what does this have to do with Jesus in the Temple, or with the relationships between husbands and wives, children and parents?

When he was twelve, just on the cusp of maturity, Jesus stayed behind in the Temple when his parents went up from Jerusalem after the festival. It was a good while before they realized he was missing—you can picture the crowds of relations and friends on a joyful journey—they most likely thought the growing boy was off somewhere with his pals and would come along shortly. Of course, when he did not turn up, they became more than worried and returned to Jerusalem.

The gospel reports it took three days to find him. We might find the reference to three days strikes a chord in our memories, recalling Jesus' death, burial, and resurrection. Here his parents find the young Jesus quite alive, asking questions of the teachers, who were amazed at his grasp of the Scriptures.

But, what about his parents? Why would Jesus leave Mary and Joseph in a panic? Exegetes have turned this story upside down trying to reconcile Jesus' duty to his mother and father with his call to live the prophecy of Scripture. We can just imagine Mary, overjoyed and perhaps a little angry. We can imagine Jesus, innocently stating his reason for being where he was.

In all our lives, the tension never ends. St. Ignatius of Loyola speaks of choosing between or among "goods." He does not mean physical items, but ways of proceeding that are, or appear to be, equally good. Robert Frost's poem "The Road Not Taken" echoes the problem of choice. The traveler cannot take both roads; he leaves one for another day, even knowing he will never return. His choice, whichever it is, "has made all the difference."

Jesus chose to be in the Temple. His parents chose to return for him. He then began to explain who he was, exactly as we might expect a young man entering adulthood to do. But, was he "obedient" to his parents? How could he leave them so filled with anxiety?

Fact is, that happens in many, if not most lives. At some point we need to be obedient to who we are; we need to choose a path; we need to leave our parents (and perhaps their dreams for us) to strike out on our own.

A GRACE FOR TODAY

Lord, help me strike a balance in my choices.

Nunc Dimittis

1 JOHN 2:3–11; LUKE 2:22–35

*It had been revealed to [Simeon] by the Holy Spirit that he
should not see death before he had seen the Christ of the Lord....
and when the parents brought in the child Jesus to perform the
custom of the law in regard to him, he took him into his arms
and blessed God, saying: "Lord, now let your servant go in
peace; your word has been fulfilled: my own eyes have seen the
salvation which you prepared in the sight of every people, a light
to reveal you to the nations and the glory of your people Israel."*

LUKE 2:26–32

The timelines get a little confusing here. The ceremony of con-
secrating the firstborn to the Lord typically took place at least
forty days after the child's birth, at the time of the Mother's purification. The church celebrates the feast of the Presentation on
February 2, forty days after Christmas.

But in today's gospel, we see Mary and Joseph in simplicity and poverty offering "a pair of turtledoves or two young pi-
geons" as they consecrate their child to God. The Levitical law
they followed says the poor may sacrifice small birds in place of
the required lamb.

I wonder how they felt. There are so many ways we separate
the poor in our societies. Some time ago, I sat on the stage at a
girls' high school graduation—I was the commencement speak-
er—and noticed all the girls were wearing white shoes to match

their white academic gowns. As they walked past me, one by one, I began to notice their shoes. Some were leather, some plastic; some were fashionable, some were simple bedroom slippers. I knew, and felt deeply, that some of these high school graduates just did not have the money to buy white shoes for their big day.

I wonder if Mary and Joseph felt that way, showing themselves simple and as poor that afternoon in the Temple. They must have had to swallow hard and walk in, heads held high, to present their baby to God.

How wonderful the way that Simeon greets them, how he cradles the child and prays aloud what we now call the Nunc Dimittis, Simon's beautiful prayer of abandonment, which the church uses in Night Prayer. In fact, in a very deep way we are all called to be simple and poor, to abandon ourselves to sleep and to pray: "Lord, now let your servant go in peace; your word has been fulfilled…"

So often it has. Sometimes it has not. Evening is the time we gather the graces of the day and give thanks—for the ongoing graces of our time and our talents, for the small and large daily graces. The canticle is one of simple gratitude and trust by the old man who had God's promise he would not die until he had seen the one who was to come, the Messiah. As Mary and Joseph looked on, Simeon held the child, and in his arms the Spirit's promise to him was fulfilled. We might be now writing thank you notes for gifts large and small. No matter how much or how little we received, no matter how much or how little we have, we give thanks. Gratitude is the key to our relationship with God and with all around us.

A GRACE FOR TODAY

Lord, grant me the grace to be grateful.

Prophecy

1 John 2:12–17; Luke 2:36–40

There was a prophetess, Anna,...She never left the temple,
but worshiped night and day with fasting and prayer.
And coming forward at that very time, she gave thanks
to God and spoke about the child to all who were awaiting
the redemption of Jerusalem.

LUKE 2:36– 38

The day Simeon held the child in the Temple, the 84-year-old prophetess Anna was there. She too had much to say about Jesus.

Anna, whose husband died many years before, spent her life in prayer. She was a woman who could read hearts, who could sense the dreams of those around her. She spent her days in the temple. Now Mary and Joseph are there with the child whose miraculous birth is kept in secret—for now—yet who already is acknowledged as the One who was to come.

And Anna was telling anyone who would listen about Jesus: "She gave thanks to God and spoke about the child to all who were awaiting the redemption of Jerusalem."

There must have been tremendous rejoicing, even silently, within the hearts of those who were also waiting, and who believed. The promised one is present. The promise of the one present cannot be refused. God is so very good!

Waiting brings conflicting emotions. You know the feeling.

You watch out the window, waiting for your child to walk down the block after school, or to arrive for his or her first Christmas vacation after being away at college, or for a loved one to arrive in from the airport. All sorts of thoughts collide—fear, certainly, mixed with joyful hope. We passed the lovely season of Advent in this joyful waiting, sometimes mixed with the anxiety of too much to do and no time (and perhaps not enough money) to do it.

We can surely recall how the anxiety rose in Mary's heart as Simeon spoke in yesterday's gospel: "Behold, this child is destined for the fall and rise of many in Israel, and to be a sign that will be contradicted (and you yourself a sword will pierce) so that the thoughts of many hearts may be revealed." Now Anna has reaffirmed Jesus' destiny, and he is still a baby.

The relationship between mother and child is complex. Not long ago I saw a cow give birth. She was a "first timer," as they say, and she quite clearly had no idea what was happening to her. Cows give birth lying down, and she did lie down, and she did try to push, but then she would stand up again and look for something to eat. Finally the calf's two hooves appeared, then the nose, but she was not pushing and so the calf had to be pulled out of her. Usually, the mother will take to the child, but in this case she just lay there, then stood, but did not go near her newborn bull. Eventually, the calf stood and tried to suck, but she was having none of it.

Other cows were well attending their newborns, but this one just was not. It was just so sad.

I think the new mother cow was totally concerned about herself. She was feeding herself with hay, even as her own calf was trying to suck, and she was trying to get away from the calf.

You are not like that. Mary was certainly not like that. She had her child, she loved her child, and even though the Temple professionals were warning that she would meet with deep sorrow as the child grew, she held her child perhaps even tighter and loved him perhaps even more.

A GRACE FOR TODAY

Lord, help me fall in love and stay there.

Accepting the light

1 John 2:18–21; John 1:1–18

A man named John was sent from God. He came for testimony,
to testify to the light, so that all might believe through him.
He was not the light, but came to testify to the light.
The true light, which enlightens everyone, was coming
into the world. John 1:6-9

As the old year draws to a close, we hear the beginning of John's gospel proclaimed again. This prologue announces the coming of Christ—the Word made flesh—whose birth we celebrated just about a week ago.

Before the church revised the liturgy of the Eucharist, the prologue to John's gospel was proclaimed at the end of every Mass. It still concludes the Tridentine Mass: "In principio erat Verbum et Verbum erat apud Deum et Deus erat Verbum."

In the beginning was the Word, and the Word was with God and the Word was God. What does this mean? How do words work? What is the Word made flesh?

I think we can understand that words actually make things present. We remember events, scenes from our own lives, through words. We read or hear words, and these help create emotions in us. We have sacred words and we have banned words; we have sad words and we have joyful words.

Now, John is saying he is testifying to the light, and that light, a true light, was coming to the world. We know that in the cycle of

101

the liturgy, the light, that light, dawned on Christmas morn.

I believe Christ's light shines in our hearts and minds whenever we allow it to enter. I also believe that when we get a little too self-preoccupied, we close the shutters and the light cannot enter.

Let me give you an example. I remember riding on a subway once in Boston—they call it the "T"—feeling downright miserable. The details by now are cloudy, but the recitative was a regular: "I failed." "I was rejected." "I am no good." I was so involved in my own personal heartbreak that I was not aware of my surroundings. Somewhere, I think between Kenmore Square and Park Street, someone reached into my pocketbook. I was lucky. He, or she, got only my checkbook—no money, no identification, no keys.

The moral of this story is not that we should ignore hurts. We need to attend to what troubles us. The moral of the story is that this event took place just before Christmas, when lights were all around me. People were jostling their loads of Christmas gifts. The sounds of bell ringers and musicians flowed into open doors as the trolley cars moved from stop to stop.

Yet I was pretty out of it. I was not caught up in the fact of Christmas, or that people were rushing home to friends and family, or that joy surrounded me. No. I was stuck in my own little world feeling miserable and, quite frankly, not giving a darn about anyone or anything around me. So I lost my checkbook.

In fact, I lost much more. I lost those moments on the T. I lost the opportunity to see the musician's smiles, to hear the bell ringer's laughter. I was so enveloped in my own darkness that I could not see the light of Christ in the faces around me.

I think of this story as the year ends, and the coming year invites me to open my eyes in wonder as the miracle of Christmas unfolds.

A GRACE FOR TODAY

Lord, grant me the grace to see your light.

A new era!

NUMBERS 6:22–27; GALATIANS 4:4–7; LUKE 2:16–21

The shepherds...made known the message that had been told
them about this child. All who heard it were amazed....
And Mary kept all these things, reflecting on them in her heart.

LUKE 2:17–19

The first of the year is a day of great—although often subdued—celebration, following the excitement of the night before. In many places of the world the New Year is ushered in by midnight bursts of fireworks, popped champagne corks, music, and cheers.

Restaurants and many homes have traded the reds and greens of Christmas for sparkling white, silver, and gold decorations to mark the turn of the calendar and perhaps of a new leaf.

We make resolutions for the New Year—to lose weight, stop smoking, perhaps to be kinder, work harder, or even take more rest.

We seem to have gotten the message: the Christ is born (as the shepherds are announcing in today's gospel) and the world has embarked on a new era.

In some parts of the world, today is still a day the church requires us to attend Mass. Most parishes recognize that this can be a difficult squeeze, between getting enough sleep and getting out to the family brunch or early dinner. So often there is just one Mass in the parish, maybe at 10:00 A.M. or 11:00 A.M., and the day's true celebration of Eucharist comes at a family gathering.

It is also Mary's day. The feast of the motherhood of Mary moved some time ago from October 11 (coincidentally, the date the Second Vatican Council opened) to January 1. I think as well it is a special day for all mothers. Consider: the child is born, the shepherds announced the birth, both Simeon and Anna predicted his greatness in the Temple, and now Mary is left to raise the boy Jesus. With Joseph, she will teach him how to become a faithful and kind Jewish man. Think of her life now, as the gospel relates: "And Mary kept all these things, reflecting on them in her heart."

In a way, we are all Mary today. There is a new year. We have new life of our own. We hold it; we cherish it; we need to nurture it and determine to give it away. What will we do to protect what we have, to love it as a gift, to help it grow, and finally, to share it with the world?

I think the most difficult part of opportunity and promise is that we tend to hold it too close. Too often we are afraid of making a mistake, and so rather than take the leap, we do nothing. Yet what do we gain by doing nothing, by hiding our talents, as it were?

Whatever her choices, we can be sure that Mary was not a "helicopter" mother, as the phrase goes, hovering over Jesus' every move, second-guessing every one of her own choices, keeping him so close that he could not grow to be the man we know he was and is.

We have the same choices in our own life, for us and for those whom we love.

A GRACE FOR TODAY

Lord, grant me the grace to live this New Year.

Being you

1 John 2:22–28; John 1:19–28

"Who are you?" John 1:19

Today's gospel retells John's encounter with the priests and Levites who asked if he was the Christ. "Who are you?" they asked. John says he is not the promised one and again points to Jesus, the child born in Bethlehem whose public ministry is by this time known. John affirms that Jesus is the Christ, and in so doing he underscores the facts both of Jesus' humanity and of Jesus' divinity.

Of course, we know that the facts of Jesus' humanity and divinity, along with the mystery of the Trinity, are the main problems of Christianity. Scholars and others have spilled gallons of ink defending or debunking what the church teaches.

Today's saints, Basil and Gregory, faced the same questions about Jesus in their fourth-century churches. Close friends, each became a bishop in the East, Basil in Caesarea and Gregory in Constantinople. As bishops, they faced and argued against the heresy of Arianism—the assertion that Jesus Christ was created human and did not share equally in the divinity of God. Arianism essentially denies the divinity of Christ.

In many ways, John's gospel, and John himself, answer the Arian heresy quite directly. John's gospel is the most philosophical of the four. I sometimes think he is a little confusing, that he uses more words than necessary to explain the simple facts of Jesus' life, death, and resurrection. In fact, I almost think he sounds a little defensive at times.

We all get like that. What does it mean to answer the question "Who are you?" At any given moment anyone can (and would) answer in a different way, mainly because we routinely identify ourselves in relation to someone or something else.

Who am I? It is an interesting and essentially unending question. Am I my profession? Am I a neighbor, a relative, a friend? Am I the sum of my experiences and memories? Am I all of these?

When John answers the question, he does so negatively. He says who he is not. He is not the Christ. We can answer in the same way: we are not the Christ. But John knows that, in addition to whatever he might consider as his profession, his relationships, and the sum of his experiences and memories, the reason for his being is to point to Jesus as the Christ.

That, I believe, is true for all of us. It certainly was true for Basil and Gregory. They were who they were; they knew who they were; but the totality of their very beings was devoted to witnessing to the humanity and divinity of Christ. They did it in their own ways throughout their lives, as sons, as friends, as monks, as priests, and as bishops. As their lives unfolded, the complexities of their personal vocations became clearer and clearer.

We all face the same question. What am I to do with my life? I certainly asked it of myself. There are a number of vocations I dismissed early on: ballerina, astronaut, race car driver, professional tennis player. The list goes on; you have your own. Yet even in the ups and downs of ongoing determinations and decisions of how to spend the precious days we have, we can see each choice as a plus or a minus for our bottom-line vocation, which is to witness Christ every day.

A GRACE FOR TODAY

Lord, grant me the grace to choose who I am.

Epiphany!

Isaiah 60:1–6; Ephesians 3:2–3a, 5–6; Matthew 2:1–12

Magi from the east arrived in Jerusalem, saying, "Where is the newborn king of the Jews? We saw his star at its rising and have come to do him homage."...They were overjoyed at seeing the star, and on entering the house they saw the child with Mary his mother. They prostrated themselves and did him homage. Then they opened their treasures and offered him gifts of gold, frankincense, and myrrh. MATTHEW 2:1–2, 10–11

Epiphany is a wonderful feast. Many countries celebrate it as "Three Kings Day," often on January 6. In some parts of Europe, priests bless frankincense, gold, and chalk. Then the chalk is used to mark the doors of churches and homes with the letters of the first names of the three kings: Caspar, Melchior, and Balthasar. C+M+B can also mean "Christus mansionem benedicat," May Christ bless this house. Other cultures have other traditions. In parts of South America, children leave shoes outside, along with grass and water for the three kings' camels, and receive a gift in the morning.

Too often we overlook Epiphany for what it is. These three men traveled some distance following a star and found the child Jesus. They knew—as they went and surely when they got there—exactly what had happened. They brought what they considered most precious—gold, surely, and frankincense, a special incense used in the Temple in Jerusalem, and myrrh, a sweet-smelling oil with healing properties.

How can we think of these gifts, except as signifying Jesus' life and death? How else to we signify kingship but with gold? How do we honor God except with incense? How do we balm injuries except with myrrh?

But there is more to the story. How do these items play in our lives, within our own epiphanies, within our own realizations of what is and what is to come?

What use is gold? I can recall asking the man who ran the copying center at my university many years ago: What is the use of money? What does it matter whether we have any or not, so long as we can get along? He gave a very interesting answer. He said you need money in case you ever need a doctor or a lawyer. A friend told me much the same not long ago. He said my car insurance seemed adequate, but my insurance company was not good, and I might still be at risk if something happened. The comments surely raised anxiety, but the opposite is also true, at least in my own life. By that I mean, I have always had enough and have avoided financial tragedy. So far.

What about incense? We rarely see incense in church except at funerals. Its use in the funeral Mass is twofold: to cense the altar and the casket is to purify them, and the smoke rising upward joins our own prayers for the dead.

And myrrh? Scientists today are investigating the healing powers of myrrh, and research promises to justify its ancient uses. The kings brought it to the child Jesus, the soldier at the crucifixion raised wine mixed with myrrh. It is used in the anointing oil for the healing sacrament of the sick.

Which of these do we need? Of course we need some "gold," to manage and sustain our daily lives. If we know incense as metaphor for prayer, we can certainly understand how much we need it. And, if we know myrrh as symbol of our need for healing in so many ways, we will see how it fits in as well.

What is our epiphany? I think it is to recognize that the three kings brought Jesus what life needs every day, and that by his teaching we are able to recognize the proper use for each.

A GRACE FOR TODAY
Lord, grant me the graces of Epiphany.

Seeing Christ

1 John 3:22–4:6; Matthew 4:12–17, 23–25

He went around all of Galilee, teaching in their synagogues,
proclaiming the gospel of the kingdom, and curing every disease
and illness among the people. His fame spread to all of Syria,
and they brought to him all who were sick with various diseases
and racked with pain, those who were possessed, lunatics,
and paralytics, and he cured them. And great crowds
from Galilee, the Decapolis, Jerusalem, and Judea,
and from beyond the Jordan followed him.

MATTHEW 4:23–25

Around this time, the church in the United States recalls Elizabeth Bayley Seton, the late eighteenth-, early nineteenth-century foundress of the Sisters of Charity. She was the daughter of a physician, wife of a businessman, and mother of five children who lived an early social ministry in her circles. As a widow, in 1809 she opened a girls' academy and soon founded the Sisters of Charity in the state of Maryland.

There was a lot of healing needed in Elizabeth's America. Capitalism was on the rise, but it was still a simple preindustrial nation, and as Elizabeth embarked on her religious mission, the economy was poor. She founded orphanages and schools in New York and Cincinnati. Her charism grew. She cared for the poor. Many joined her, and her fame spread.

Think of Jesus in today's gospel: "His fame spread to all of

Syria, and they brought to him all who were sick ... and he cured them."

Jesus' miracles are echoed in Elizabeth's work. She was not a physician—her sisters would later found hospitals—but she healed more than bodies. So too with Jesus. We know the wonderful stories recounted in the gospels of Jesus healing people. His commanding the paralytic man to take up his mat and walk is a startling example of both his abilities and the man's faith.

But what can we mere mortals do? How can we help suffering people? I am not sure it is such a difficult question. Very few of us are called to begin major movements or to found institutions. Yet chances are there is a neighbor or friend in terrible pain this very minute. We may also be in terrible pain. But I have learned quite profitably that when I pay attention to the wounds of others I tend to forget my own and, once I can return to my own self-concerns, they seem somehow lessened.

As much as I have read about saints and founders, about martyrs and great doctors of the church, I find in them the single strand of self-effacing love for others. Their concerns are not principally for themselves, but for those others whom they know and those others whom they do not know. They have fallen in love with the face of Christ that shines in every person they meet. That love moves them to the great lives they lead.

I think that is the key to the magnificent start Elizabeth Seton gave to the distinctly American form of religious life lived throughout the United States today. I think it is the key to our own lives as well.

A GRACE FOR TODAY

Lord, let me see Christ's face in everyone I meet.

Teaching and Learning

1 John 4:7–10; Mark 6:34–44

*When Jesus saw the vast crowd, his heart was moved with pity
for them, for they were like sheep without a shepherd; and he
began to teach them many things.* MARK 6:34

The hillsides of Galilee are harsh and unforgiving. Steep in
many places, their rocks and scrub give little relief to the walk-
er and surely gave less to those who sat listening to Jesus. They
hungered for many things, and Jesus gave them food in this telling of the story by Mark.

But first he fed their souls.

Shortly after the New Year, the Church remembers Saint
John Neumann, who came to New York from what is now the
Czech Republic to begin his priestly ministry, first in New York,
then in Pennsylvania and Maryland as a Redemptorist priest.
At 41, he became the bishop of Philadelphia.

Neumann, who spoke six languages, established national parishes in his diocese to feed the souls and bodies of
Philadelphia's many immigrants. He began the nation's first di-
ocesan school system.

Say what you want about Catholic schools, in nineteenth-century America, they gave the poor a chance. Some institutes of
women religious were already in Philadelphia when Neumann
arrived; he founded another and encouraged others to come. In
retrospect, while he is credited with the formation of a coordi-

nated system of Catholic education, he could never have done it without the self-sacrifice of thousands of sisters who toiled to actually build it. Nor would the thousands upon thousands of poor children in Philadelphia in Neumann's time have learned a thing unless the sisters were watching out for their bodily needs as well.

If you picture today's immigrants, searching for new lives even in the lands Neumann left, you can well appreciate how necessary food is to learning—whether learning a new language or skill, or learning more about religion. Jesus knew this so well, and so did the sisters who worked in Neumann's school system.

In rich countries, we think it a great hardship to miss a meal, and we happily attend church services whenever we want. Yet the United Nations says 795 million people—one of every nine in the world—face food insecurity. We like to say people hunger for the word of God, but the simple fact is that people are just plain hungry.

Teaching and learning cannot happen in destitution. So, what to do? Do we stop talking about Jesus? Do we stop spreading the word of God?

I think it facile to say that all our energies need be devoted to world poverty. I think it equally facile to say that all our energies need be devoted to evangelization. To me, Mark's words are central: "his heart was moved with pity for them."

The compassionate people in my life—mostly, if not exclusively women—have "fed" me and given me the ability to feed myself, both bodily and spiritually. The secular subjects sisters taught me gave me the ability to earn a living. The ways the sisters taught gave me an example of how hear the gospel and to live it.

A GRACE FOR TODAY

Lord, grant me the grace to teach and to learn.

Be not afraid

1 John 4:11–18; Mark 6:45–52

When they saw him walking on the sea, they thought
it was a ghost and cried out. They had all seen him
and were terrified. But at once he spoke with them,
"Take courage, it is I, do not be afraid!"
He got into the boat with them and the wind died down.
They were completely astounded. They had not understood
the incident of the loaves. On the contrary,
their hearts were hardened. MARK 6:49-52

The early seventeenth-century Dutch painter Rembrandt van
Rijn recreated the scene in this gospel in his "The Storm on the
Sea of Galilee." The painting—a genuine masterpiece—was
on display for many years in Boston's Isabella Stewart Gardner
Museum. Then it was stolen. It has never been recovered.

I think we all have travel horror stories that might match
the fierceness of a sudden storm on the Sea of Galilee. I know
myself that I have made many promises to the Lord while ap-
proaching Kennedy Airport in bad weather. The fear, of course,
is of not being in control.

However some years ago, while flying across Europe from
Germany to England, I mentioned my fears to a flight atten-
dant. Soon she returned from the cockpit—this was many
years ago—and said that Mike and Hector had invited me "up
front." Since I was in the first seat, I inquired as to what "up

front" meant. Oh, she said, they have invited you to the cockpit. Frightened or not, who would miss the chance?

As I stood at the open cockpit door, the pilots explained where we were and how the plane worked. It was cloudy, but they were able to tell me when we crossed the Rhine, when we were over France, when we approached the English Channel. Every so often they would check in with ground control, or be "handed off" from one control area to another. The instructions they received were curt and precise: turn left this many degrees; climb to this altitude. But all one of them did was move a little knob, and the plane did the rest. The two pilots explained that when they entered the destination into the airplane's computers, it pretty much knew what to do on its own. They monitored, and took over completely whenever necessary.

I have not been afraid flying since. I say this for many reasons. First, I am completely convinced that it is better for Mike and Hector and their colleagues to be listening to ground control and turning the knobs. Second, my cinematic ideas of pilots shouting to one another "flaps down," "copy that," evaporated in the cockpit that day. Third, I recognized, standing there, how foolish I was to think I might be able to control the situation on my own.

That is the moral of the story. When the St. Louis Jesuits recorded their song "Be Not Afraid," I am quite sure they had me and many other control-prone folks in mind. Not that I am marching across barren deserts or spending much time on raging waters, but you know as well as I do that our lives metaphorically include these very dangers, and we tend to fear them even when we are not in them.

But we are not in complete control of every single thing that happens around us. I try to trust that God's people act on God's behalf to keep me safe—whether in an airplane or on the sea or anywhere else—and ask for the grace to not have a hardened heart, but to trust.

So I tend to try not to borrow trouble. I tend to try not to be afraid.

A GRACE FOR TODAY

Lord, grant me the grace to trust your care for me.

Bring glad tidings

1 John 4:19—5:4; Luke 4:14–22

Jesus returned to Galilee....He came to Nazareth, where he had grown up, and went according to his custom into the synagogue on the sabbath day. He stood up to read and was handed a scroll of the prophet Isaiah. He unrolled the scroll and found the passage where it was written: The Spirit of the Lord is upon me, because he has anointed me to bring glad tidings to the poor. He has sent me to proclaim liberty to captives and recovery of sight to the blind, to let the oppressed go free, and to proclaim a year acceptable to the Lord. LUKE 4:14, 16-19

Nazareth sits snugly in the Galilean hills about ninety miles north of Jerusalem, ten or fifteen miles west of the Sea of Galilee. During Jesus' time, it was a tiny backwater village.

Picture Jesus, now back in his hometown. The Sabbath comes. He goes to the synagogue. When his turn comes, he reads Isaiah's words with new meaning: The Spirit of the Lord is upon me, because he has anointed me to bring glad tidings to the poor....

That is what he has been doing all along.

These post-Christmas days find us enjoying a little more light, as the sun rises a little earlier and sets a little later each day. Imagine the burst of interior light listening to Jesus read from Isaiah. Imagine how those around you rustle in recognition. Imagine your own feelings, there in the presence of the promised one, as he proclaims the reasons for his being.

We are just past Epiphany, but every day grants an opportunity for a new epiphany. For me, the recognition of Jesus as the Christ is a daily event in a world that so despises the poor. We live surrounded by noise masquerading as music, nonsense masquerading as speech, foolishness masquerading as proper behavior. And it is the noisemakers and nonsensical and foolish among us who despise the poor.

There are two distinct groups: they who live the virtues of religion and they who do not. Too often the poor are looked down upon by both groups. The secular noisemakers see the poor as "losers." Too often the "religious" people among us feel somewhat the same.

I am reminded of Dorothy Day's story about waiting in a social service agency to apply for housing, I believe for someone living at her Mary House on the Lower East Side of Manhattan. After some time, an official asked Dorothy her name.

"Oh, Ms. Day," he said. "I am sorry to make you wait. I thought you were just one of the clients."

That is not the message of glad tidings to the poor. That is officiousness masquerading as social service.

It happens every day. In small ways and large, we judge people. For whatever reasons, we see ourselves as either higher or lower than the stranger. We have more education, they have less money, we have more friends, and so it goes.

I think when we are trying to understand Jesus' message, really trying to hear him proclaim Isaiah that day in the synagogue, we need to look into our own hearts and minds to see if his light stings our memories.

It is very hard to live as a highly educated and financially secure person surrounded by friends and family and not somehow feel ever so slightly superior to some others.

I think what we fail to recognize is that poverty has many forms, and the one before us with less education or money or friends or family—any or all of these—lives the poverty Jesus intends us not only to heal, but also to respect.

A GRACE FOR TODAY

Lord, grant me the grace to respect the poor.

Healing

1 John 5:5–13; Luke 5:12–16

*Jesus stretched out his hand, touched him, and said, "I do will it.
Be made clean." And the leprosy left him immediately. Then
he ordered him not to tell anyone, but....The report about him
spread all the more, and great crowds assembled to listen to him
and to be cured of their ailments, but he would withdraw
to deserted places to pray.* LUKE 5:13-16

Everybody hurts. Not everybody has leprosy or any of its modern
equivalents, but everybody hurts and needs some sort of healing.

The problem of leprosy, as you know, is that aside from its
physical trials, it made its sufferers outcasts. Despite the fact
that the disease is not that contagious and is curable, people
with leprosy are still separated from the general population in
parts of China, India, and Africa.

The man who approached Jesus took a big risk. So did Jesus,
in two ways. First, Jesus touched the man. Then Jesus told the
man, once cured, to tell no one.

Well, that didn't work. Can you imagine? How did this simple preacher cure by touch? Could the cured man contain his
joy? Could you?

What happened when you were "cured"? I know in my own
life I have had both physical and spiritual healing. I have had my
share of orthopedic excitement, with surgeries, casts, braces,
physical therapy, and the like. They each and all have taken up a

lot of my time, but these injuries have been helped toward healing by the patient attention of physicians and other professionals. So what do I do? I share my gratitude with the world—or at least with my world—and recommend my healers to others.

I think that is what was going on in Jesus' day. Word spread. Here is a man who, by touch and prayer, can heal. Here is a man who asks for nothing. Here is a man who tells his disciples not to accept any payment.

But I do not think no-charge healing is what drew people to Jesus. The fact of the matter is, he healed, he cured, and he asked that these miracles—for that is what they are—be kept secret. No self-promoter he!

I see Jesus' humility in the light of his great power echoed in some of the spiritual directors I have encountered in my life. We are accustomed to the science of medicine and its rational methods of healing. But the grace to practice well the art of spiritual direction is always borne humbly by those who minister so. The ministry is so intimate that professionally trained directors never speak about their directees, ever. I have known it as such a deeply graced ministry that I rarely, if ever, mention the names of the men and women who have walked with me in my own spiritual journey. If I do, it is only to my closest friends.

I think the challenge of being a healer—either physical or spiritual—is keeping the focus on the one who is ailing. Having said that, I think we are all healers of one sort or another. We listen to the pained troubles of our friends and families, and we offer what simple advice we can. Through it all, we know that their pain is sacred, and theirs alone, never to be shared.

A GRACE FOR TODAY

Lord, grant me the grace to heal with humility.

He must increase

1 John 5:14–21; John 3:22–30

*"So this joy of mine has been made complete. He must increase;
I must decrease."* John 3:29-30

As the Christmas season draws to a close, we find John restating a fact of Jesus that I think we can all take into our hearts and minds. He must increase. I must decrease.

That, after all, is the journey of the spiritual life. Just as the world's darkness yields to the changing season, our own darkness gradually yields to light, the light of Christ. Sometimes that light is painfully bright, and we cannot stand to look at ourselves in it. Sometimes that light is more subtle, and we seek the assistance of others to find the way.

The Christmas season draws together themes that carry us through the year. We begin in hope, we greet the birth of Jesus, and we begin to learn about him and his ministry. As we keep these themes in mind, we can better understand that the task of every Christian is to become another Christ; we can better understand that the only way to do that is by continually learning about him, his words, his ways, his works. That intimate knowledge of Jesus is what we strive for, as gift and grace, as recognition and reward.

No matter how we go about it, we must always hold close John's words as his recommendation to us on the path: He must increase. I must decrease.

That is not that easy, but it is not that hard, either. I know my own struggles, where I have wanted to be first, to be best, or to be noticed were not in God's plan for my life. It has taken quite some time for me to realize that what God wants of me is what God wants of everyone: to simply be who I am in Christ's light. That has meant a lot of giving up what I wanted, places I wanted to go, things I thought I should have or even deserved.

I think I have finally figured out that whatever light I shine on anything is not coming from me. Whatever light I shine is merely reflecting the light of Christ as it shines—lovingly— on me. That is not to deny my talents and training. No, what I mean by that is that with God's grace and, as the saying goes, a little help from my friends, I have found my place and only ask daily that Christ might increase in the world.

A GRACE FOR TODAY

Lord, grant me the grace to mirror your light.

With you I am well pleased

YEAR A: ISAIAH 42:1–4, 6–7; ACTS 10:34–38; MATTHEW 3:13–17

YEAR B: ISAIAH 55:1–11; 1 JOHN 5:1–9; MARK 1:7–11

YEAR C: ISAIAH 40:1–5, 9–11; TITUS 2:11–14, 3:4–7;

LUKE 3:15–16, 21–22

After all the people had been baptized and Jesus also had been baptized and was praying, heaven was opened and the Holy Spirit descended upon him in bodily form like a dove. And a voice came from heaven, "You are my beloved Son; with you I am well pleased." LUKE 3:21-22

The early church had a long process of catechesis before baptism, and the ceremony itself eventually developed into quite a complex liturgy. But the earliest baptisms were rather simple. Today's gospel recounts Jesus' baptism in the Jordan. Jewish practice included "Tvilah," a repeatable purification by immersion in water. John the Baptist adopted this "baptism" as a central part of his work and ministry. It is likely that Jesus was undergoing this ritual at John's hands when the dove descended upon him.

There is a special quality to water. I know myself the feeling of being enveloped by it in the ocean or a bay. Water, natural water, heals and holds us up, calms and cools. It washes away whatever is on us; it refreshes and soothes the soul and the body.

Christians take baptism as the first sacrament of initiation. It makes sense for someone to be wholly cleansed before reception into the church. The grace of the sacrament cleanses whatever sins the catechumen brings to baptism. Baptism frees the baptized child of original or ancestral sin. In Christ the newly baptized are truly new creations.

Yet even without belief in the grace of this or any sacrament, I think we can hold dear the times in our own lives when something has been forgiven and then forgotten. That, to me, is the promise of baptism and the promise of a life in Christ. It is that promise that keeps me going, and probably you as well.

As the church's liturgical season of Christmas comes to a close today, I think it well to recognize that tomorrow begins what the church calls "Ordinary Time." It is a wonderful name for most of the church year, and it is a wonderful name for our lives. We mostly live ordinary lives, day in, day out. Our journeys can be difficult, can be exciting, can be troubled, and can be wonderful.

Saints ancient and contemporary help us mark our journeys by speaking about theirs. We mark our own journeys with calendars and diaries. We reverence ourselves and the life of Christ within us by holding our own stories sacred. Sometimes we share our stories with friends, with relatives, or with spiritual directors. Most times we hold our stories close.

I think the key to living as baptized Christians is to recognize that as we live our own stories, we recall as well our own baptisms. Without a doubt, at your baptism the dove descended, and the voice of God said: "This is my beloved, in whom I am well pleased."

May God hold you close on the journey.

A GRACE FOR TODAY
Lord, let me always know I am your beloved.